INTERACTIVE
PLAY GUIDE

CRAIG OGILVIE

Interactive play guide

INTERACTIVE
PLAY GUIDE

CRAIG OGILVIE

First Stone Publishing

The Old Hen House, St Martin's Farm, Zeals, Warminster, Wiltshire, BA12 6NZ

Printed and bound in China through Printworks International.

All rights reserved. No part of this work may be reproduced, in any form or by any means, electronic or mechanical, including photocopying, recording or by any information storage and retrieval system, without the prior written permission of the publisher.

Copyright © First Stone Publishing Company 2017.

The 'he' pronoun is used throughout this book instead of the rather impersonal 'it', however no gender bias is intended.

ISBN: 978-1-910488-34-8

Photography:
Tiffani Ogilvie

CONTENTS

The Discovery..6

Interaction for Invincibility......................12

Non Verbal Communication...................30

Toy Selection..58

Energy's Effects......................................72

Relationship Building.............................96

Activating The Toy................................106

Control During Interactive Play..............130

Teaching And Timing............................154

Incremental Steps To Interactivity.............162

Vocalisation Consideration....................176

Every Dog Is Unique.............................184

Love The Journey..................................188

THE DISCOVERY

It was a cold winter's afternoon in late 2010; my feeling of excitement was only matched by the feeling of anticipation that accompanied it. I was travelling to a foreign country, setting out on a brand new adventure.

One thing was certain; this wasn't going to be an average trip. The purpose of my journey was to undergo tests to see if was suitable to be bitten by highly trained dogs on a regular basis...

In fact, it's not as crazy as it sounds. I was en route to a Mondioring sports club in France to see if I had what it takes to become a Mondioring decoy.

Mondioring is a dog sport where handlers train their dogs to be tested in obedience, agility and in the biting and apprehension of a trained and licensed person. The best comparison is that the training and tests are very similar to the police dog programme.

I bombarded my travelling companion with questions, and his polite, articulate answers gave me some idea of what I could expect. He was a chance acquaintance but, in time, he would become a great role model and mentor in my dog training career. I have always been completely obsessed with dogs, which I credit to spending my childhood with my Grandad, and his service dogs.

Up until that cold afternoon, most of my time had been spent solving dog behavioural problems, training dogs, studying dogs, talking about dogs and writing about dogs. Can you spot the trend?

I had always taken a special interest in the training of police dogs, thanks to my Grandad, and this led to my involvement with Mondioring.

The first trip turned out to be a success and resulted in countless trips to Europe to be trained as a Mondioring decoy. The training was intense and challenging; to get my decoy's licence I had to pass a demanding examination that consisted of a physical fitness test, a practical skills test and a theory test, given in French.

The commitment was total, but I loved every moment of it. My role not only involved acting as a decoy, I was also responsible for training dogs in the techniques required for biting exercises in competition.

My initial learning came while I was training to be a Mondioring decoy.

So not only was I learning the complexities of a new sport, I was also training dogs of different types, with different needs. It was an unparalleled experience, and I couldn't have been happier.

That was until another even colder afternoon in 2012. This time I was staying in a very modest but homely Mondioring clubhouse in a village called Wattrelos in Northern France.

I felt just as excited as I had on my first trip – but this time I knew what was coming. One of the team of four judges called my name in his strong, nasal French accent, and I jumped to my feet and made my way to the front of the room.

The committee members were lined up, and as I passed each member I shook hands in turn. The last in the row was the President of the club, and as we shook hands he handed me my licence – I had passed! This moment was particularly special because I was the only person from the UK to have ever received this accreditation.

Since getting my licence, I have travelled all over Europe training and testing dogs to Championship level, which has been an immensely rewarding, experience. The competitions were great fun but my true love has always been with training; it was while training dogs for Mondioring that I made my big discovery.

It did not take me long to realise that I produced the best results when I trained the dogs to see the biting as part of a big game. I built good relationships with all of the dogs I trained, and I treated the padded costume that is designed for the dog to bite as one big toy – they loved it! The result was happy, motivated dogs that loved the game and loved the training.

The results were consistent regardless of the dog's shape or size, or breed type. When working with puppies and younger dogs, I noticed that the desire for this type of game, which starts

My big discovery was that play builds relationships and establishes real communication with dogs.

interactive play guide | 9

off with a tug toy or a rolled up tea towel, had amazing benefits. It allowed me to build relationships, increase confidence, motivate and communicate with the dogs. I remember thinking, how can this be?

Most of the time the reward was an old tea towel that had no value. In fact, the tea towel was immaterial; the reason the dogs loved the game was because of the whole interactive play experience I was creating. After working with a wide range of youngsters, I knew my approach would work for adult dogs too, which it did with great success.

So I thought: there is no reason why this discovery has to be kept a secret among handlers of working dogs. I wanted to share the experience with as many dog lovers as possible.

I started to use my take on interactive play with my behavioural clients as a way to build better relationships with their dogs. It proved to be an amazing exercise activity that stimulated the dogs mentally and physically – and they loved it.

It worked equally well with my training clients, helping them to motivate and reward their dogs in training – and it was all viewed as one big game.

Soon, through word of mouth, I received invitations to hold seminars and workshops on the interactive play experience and it was not long before everyone was talking about it.

I was captivated by how much everyone was benefitting from creating their own interactive play experiences and loving the whole journey.

A light bulb moment came when a few people that couldn't make it to my workshops contacted me for advice on how to create their own interactive play experience.

After responding to lots of messages, I started to think about the best way to share this information with as many dog lovers as possible.

After a lot of thought, I came up with the INTERACTIVE acronym system, which is the foundation of this book and my online courses.

Each letter of INTERACTIVE makes up a chapter of this book and serves as an individual lesson. I can promise two things: interactive play will enhance your relationship with your dog – and you will have the very best of fun along the way!

My mission is to spread the interactive play message far and wide.

NTERACTION FOR INVINCIBILITY

When we play with our dogs, it is the way in which we interact with them that is of paramount importance. It is the interactive element that makes or breaks a dog's drive and desire to play, so this needs to be your focus when you are creating an interactive play experience.

In this chapter, I will highlight some of the common misconceptions and mistakes that can be made when you engage in play sessions with your dog. I will show you the right way to interact, offering techniques that will make the interaction as valuable to your dog as the toy itself.

I will describe how you can make your dog feel invincible during your interactive play sessions and how this feeling of invincibility can enhance his desires, drive and motivation. I will then explain how these benefits can be utilised in all the different aspects of a dog lover's life.

WHERE DO WE START?

Play sparks a great feeling of fun and excitement in both dog and handler. I must admit that interacting with a dog in this way always gets me smiling, no matter what dog I am working with. However, problems often arise when we transfer our mental excitement to the physical activity as, more often than not, we are considerably stronger than our dogs.

To be physically boisterous with our dogs during play, albeit

It is important to get play off on the right footing.

Interactive play guide | 13

unintentionally, is a common and easy mistake to make. But it can have a major effect on a dog's attitude, and is often the reason for depreciated drive to play, lack of desire to interact with the handler and general lack of motivation surrounding the activity.

Why is that? If a handler is too boisterous during interactive play sessions, it can make the dog feel that he is an insignificant part of the experience.

If this play experience is repeated too often, you will see significant changes in the dog: he will start to lose his desire to play, the perceived value of the toy will diminish and he may show increasing reluctance to interact with his handler. There are a number of 'mistakes' that are commonly made by handlers during the play experience which can lead to a negative outcome. They include:

- Excitedly shaking the toy while the dog is holding it in his mouth, often to the point that the dog lets go of the toy.
- Unintentionally using the toy to lift the dog until his paws are off the ground, often resulting in the dog letting go of the toy.
- Running too fast while the dog tries to hold on to the toy.
- Erratic movements when both handler and dog are holding the toy.
- Boisterous physical contact.

These are just a few examples of how we can potentially reduce a dog's desire to play, his desire to interact with his handler and consequently his desire for the interactive play experience.

If unintentional mistakes occur too often, they will have a detrimental effect on even the most playful of dogs.

A SLIPPERY SLOPE

Consider a very steep hill that is covered in slippery, plastic sheeting. A stream of oil is being pumped from the top so the oil covers the entire hill. This would undoubtedly make the hill very slippery. Now consider trying to run up the hill and, repeatedly, not getting anywhere. How many attempts would it take for you to lose the desire to run up the hill?

In just the same way, if a dog repeatedly attempts to interact during your play sessions and consistently receives nothing in return for his effort, his desire for the play experience will diminish. This can result in many different behaviours, most of which involve the dog being happier to entertain himself with a toy rather than partaking in interactive play with his handler.

This can reach a point when the dog starts to become possessive over the toy or, alternatively, he shows a complete lack of interest in toys and play in general. The question is, how do we interact with our dogs during play so that they feel invincible and love the experience?

THE EVEN TUG OF WAR

The even tug of war is part of the interaction that you share with your dog while you are both holding a toy, and this can play a big part in creating the perfect interactive play experience.

To achieve an even tug of war, the whole interactive experience needs to be very considerate of the dog. If the dog has the toy in his mouth and you are holding on to the toy, you need to enhance all of the dog's efforts, regardless of how slight they may seem. Remember, we are interacting for invincibility so we have got to make the dog *feel* invincible.

If your dog pulls very slightly on the toy, try to act as if the dog is dragging you in the direction that he is pulling. Go with the force, but keep your movement smooth and fluid, as erratic movement will hamper the experience.

In this situation, it doesn't matter if the handler is the size of a heavyweight boxer and the breed of dog is a Chihuahua. The dog needs to believe he has the strength to interact with his handler as an equal; not only that, he will start to think that he can supersede his owner's strength during the interactive play experience – and the feeling of invincibility is born.

The aim is to enhance the dog's efforts to establish an even tug of war.

THE RIGHT AMOUNT OF RESISTANCE

As this is an even tug of war, it is not enough to feed the toy into the dog's mouth in an attempt to get him to pull on the toy. This will often lead to the dog mouthing the toy excessively or releasing it altogether.

Feeding the toy to the dog in this manner can also depreciate the toy's value, as movement and resistance play a big part in an even tug of war. The best way of proceeding is to resist the dog's force ever so slightly. You can do this by pulling the toy away from your dog while you are both holding it. You need to use just enough resistance to encourage the dog to continue to pull in the opposite direction. You are now beginning to create an even tug of war. At the point when the dog pulls away, I often release my hold on the toy and let him win it as a reward for his effort.

PROUD PARADE PROCESS

Once the dog has won the toy, I use a very light training lead with no handle that is approximately 1.5 metres in length, and attach it to either a soft flat collar or a harness, depending on what the dog is wearing. What is the reason for this?

Again, it is all about transferring a feeling of power and invincibility to the dog. Over the years, I have worked with lots of different dogs and I have noticed a commonality that can often show itself during interactive play sessions. In so many of these play sessions, the dog has associated his handler with his toy being taken away from him.

This often results in the dog becoming possessive of the toy so he will do his best to get away from his handler to take sole possession of his prize. To counteract this, I have invented something which I call the proud parade process. When the dog is on the light line and has won the toy, I suggest the handler jogs a circle, at medium pace, with the dog holding the toy in his mouth. This allows the dog to parade proudly with his newly-won prize.

Rather than running away to entertain himself with the toy, or giving up the moment he has won it, the dog has a chance to show off his trophy. Attaching a lead to the dog allows this to be a smooth procedure and avoids the wasted energy and potential conflict if the dog attempts to get away. The proud parading process only has to be of short duration, but it will prove to be really beneficial in creating your interactive play experience. The time you allow for the parading process will vary depending on your dog.

For example, if you have a dog that is not inclined to hold on to the toy for very long after he has 'won' it, a five-second parading could be more than enough. On the other hand, if you have a dog that has no problems holding on to the toy, the parading process could last 30 seconds.

However, this will be very dependant on your dog, as the time spent on the parading process needs to be tailored to your dog's particular needs. In this situation, and in all the exercises outlined in this book, the aim is to adjust and adapt techniques to best suit the individual dog, thus creating a highly personalised interactive play experience.

SHARING THE MOMENT

After the parading process, encourage your dog to sit/stand by your side or in front of you, with the toy in his mouth. The position he adopts is completely dependant on what he finds most comfortable. You then place one of your hands under his jaw, allowing him to rest the weight of his jaw and head on your hand, whilst holding the toy in his mouth. You can then share

A light training lead gives you the chance to work with your dog as the interactive experience is developing.

Interactive play guide | 19

affection with your dog by slowly and calmly smoothing the top of his head from front to back. The ideal is for your dog to be happy and willing to rest his jaw in your hand while firmly holding the toy in his mouth.

He should show no signs of possessiveness, nor attempt to avoid the hand that is smoothing him. I have found that, at this point, a dog may actually lean his body into the handler and attempt to nuzzle the hand that is smoothing him.

THE PURPOSE OF THE PROUD PARADE

Are you wondering what is the point of allowing your dog to parade his trophy? This is a very good question, but it is very rarely asked during a workshop or seminar demonstrations because the dogs' behaviour speaks for them. As I mentioned earlier, I have seen a lot of dogs that associate their handler with the withdrawal of their toy. This association is usually ignited as soon as the handler releases tension from the toy.

The dog has learnt through repetition and reinforcement that this signals an end to the game. If this is repeated too often, the dog's chief desire will be to get away from the handler so he can take possession of the toy and entertain himself, rather than returning to the handler to continue the play experience.

The proud parade counter-balances this because it affirms, in the dog's mind, that just because the handler has loosened his/her grip on the toy, it does not mean that the toy will be withdrawn.

Regardless of the tension on the toy, or whether the handler lets go, the dog learns that there is more of the game to come. He is, therefore, willing to re-engage rather than take possession of the toy. Remember that the interactive play experience that you are creating should supersede the value of

Sharing the moment demonstrates mutual trust between dog and handler.

the toy as a stand-alone item. You are the creator of the most amazing experience in the world. The affection sharing process depends very much on your individual dog. For example, if you are working with a dog that has depreciated toy drive and lets go of the article as soon as it stops moving, this process could be a waste of time as the dog will almost certainly drop the toy as soon as he comes in to you.

With this type of dog, I suggest a very short parading process of perhaps a few seconds, which can be followed by the immediate reactivation of the toy to create another even tug of war interaction. This will organically increase the dog's desire to keep a hold of the toy, which will allow you to work towards a period of affection sharing. If, on the other hand, the dog is a little toy possessive and doesn't seem to enjoy the interaction process, or appears to be on a self-set mission to get the toy away from the handler as quickly as possible, I would recommend prolonging the proud parading process and dedicating more time to sharing the moment.

HOW MUCH RESISTANCE AND MOVEMENT?

How do you know how much resistance and movement to use when you are interacting with your dog? When you apply resistance and movement to the toy during interaction I suggest that it should be moderate to begin with, taking on board the following factors:

- The dog's temperament and behaviour
- His desire to play and interact with you
- His toy drive
- The physical attributes of the dog

ACTIONABLE EXAMPLES

I have worked on creating and developing interactive play experiences with numerous large breed dogs, some of which nearly equal me in weight.

Despite their size and physical strength, some of these dogs had very low natural desire to play or even show an interest in toys. At this delicate stage – when you are first igniting the desire to play – you need to be very sensitive in your handling.

If I had applied anything more than very gentle resistance and movement to the toy while the dog was holding it in his mouth,

The proud parade gives the dog a chance to feel good and counteracts his belief that you want to take away his toy.

Interactive play guide | 23

he would have simply let go of the toy. This would depreciate the value of the interaction and the dog's overall desire for the new experience. In this situation, the tension I applied to the toy was very gentle and every effort that the dog made by pulling in the even tug of war was immediately enhanced. I gave the dog the upper hand and allowed him to pull me around a bit.

Working with a dog in this way quickly developed his feeling of invincibility and increased his desire for the toy and the new interactive play experience. Because of the physical size of the dogs I was working with, it would have been an easy misconception to apply resistance and movement to the toy, but this would have caused the their desire to play to decrease rather than progress.

However, as their desire began to grow, so did the physical effort they put into the interactive play. I was then able to increase the resistance and movement in relation to the dog's development.

When I was working on the first play session, I found that if I let go of the toy completely to "let the dog win" many of the dogs would simply abandon the toy and show no further interest in it. This changed as the sessions progressed. Increasingly when I let a dog win the toy, he would hold on to it and willingly bring it back me to reinitiate the interaction.

The dogs were beginning to value the interactive experience, as being enjoyable and beneficial to them, which in effect elevated their desire for the toy and their motivation for the new experience. In all cases this was excellent progress.

In contrast to these low drive dogs whose desire for the toy play needed to be encouraged, I have also used these principles when working with smaller breeds that have elevated levels of desire for a toy, but no desire to interact with the handler.

The amount of resistance you use will depend on your dog's physical make up and his own unique personality.

The toy desire causes these dogs to pull strongly, but often erratically, doing their best to get the toy from the handler as soon as possible. At this point, most of the dogs would have been more than happy to take the toy into a corner and entertain themselves. Just because this type of dog pulls strongly does not mean that we must equal or supersede their strength output.

Instead, in cases like this, it is better to find a balance. The aim is to apply just enough resistance and movement to the toy so the dog maintains motivation to interact with you, but making sure the resistance level remains moderate to show the dog that the game is an even tug of war. The dog needs to know that he is able to supersede your strength and win the toy on a very regular basis.

This consistent experience of success will teach him that interaction with a handler increases the value of the toy and makes the experience more enjoyable than the entertainment he gains by taking the toy off on his own. This will enhance the dog's desire to interact with his handler and will begin to improve their relationship. After a very short period of time, I found that most dogs were willing to bring the toy back to me once I had let them win it.

They were keen to reinitiate the interaction as they wanted more of the play experience. This was a very positive step as the dogs began to realise that it was the interaction – and the experience we shared – that made the toy valuable.

The above examples show how different adjustments and adaptations to the resistance and movement that you apply to a toy during play sessions can successfully enhance and develop your experience.

DOGS LOVE TO PLAY

Have you ever watched two social and well-balanced dogs interact or play with each other? If you have, you will notice that their interaction often follows a set pattern. The two dogs will take turns in initiating the play, often in a very even way.

They may take turns to chase each other or you may see dogs of differing sizes, such as a German Shepherd and a Jack Russell, wrestling on the ground in such a playful and even way that it appears they are of equal strength. Taking turns in steering the terms of the play makes both dogs feel invincible at different times; this is the nature of their successful, playful interaction.

For me, the most remarkable observations have come from watching a considerate, older dog build the confidence of a puppy or juvenile dog through this play process. When observing two dogs playing, you will often see another common occurrence. If one of the two dogs taking part in the play becomes too boisterous or gets over excited and begins to break the even cycle of play, the interaction or game will end rather

A chase game between dogs will end swiftly if play becomes too boisterous.

quickly. One of the dogs will 'lose interest' in the interaction to prevent the possibility of conflict. This is worth noting because I am often told that a dog is more interested in playing with other dogs rather than interacting with his handler.

Handlers are often quick to say how much the dogs enjoy these dog-to-dog play experiences. In this situation, observation is key to learning.

If you replicate the way that two dogs interact with each other in play, partaking in a very even tug of war during which the dog is regularly capable of gaining the upper hand and winning, he will feel invincible.

If you can make this feeling of invincibility part of the experience you share with you dog, his desire to interact and play with you will grow organically. In effect, the dog needs to value the interaction with you, and the experience that you create, more than the toy itself. Your dog will learn to love the whole interactive play experience – not just one part of it.

LAST THOUGHTS ON INTERACTION FOR INVINCIBILITY

I have highlighted some of the common mistakes that can be made during play sessions and how they can have an undesirable effect on creating an interactive play experience. In addition I have shown, through observation, how to put the interaction for invincibility principles in place.

A combination of keen perception and sensitive handling will help you to create an interactive play experience that boosts your dog's toy drive, his desire to engage with you – and his feeling of invincibility. Take time to meet up and watch other dog lovers interacting with their dogs during play and see if you can spot some of the dos and dont's mentioned in this chapter. Better still, try to work as a group with a common goal of developing the interactive play experience. This will serve you extremely well as you will be able to monitor and discuss your progress, as well as helping other members of the group. Communication between you and your dog is a key part of the journey, which leads me to the next chapter...

You can introduce the interactive play experience to a puppy or work on it with an older dog.

NON-VERBAL COMMUNICATION

As people, we love to talk and interact with family and friends; talking is our primary means of communication. This often transfers to when we are interacting and communicating with our dogs. There is no doubt that vocalisation during interactive play can be an amazing experience (see Chapter 11: Vocalisation).

However in this chapter, I am discussing the art of communicating with your dog with very few words. When introducing the subject of non-verbal communication, I am often asked: 'How am I supposed to communicate with my dog without talking?' Are you wondering the same thing?

In fact, our dogs are very receptive to different forms of non-verbal communication, and the tips and techniques on activating this form of communication have worked exceptionally well for myself and for my clients in creating amazing interactive play experiences. Let's get started.

BODY LANGUAGE AND POSITIONING

Your body language and positioning during play is hugely relevant to your dog; the degree he is affected will depend on his own individual temperament. If you are working with a dog who lacks the desire to play, is nervous, or has possessive issues, you need to be especially aware of what you are doing. However, the basic techniques employed in successful non-verbal communication apply equally to all handlers who are developing the interactive play experience.

You need to open up a dialogue with your dog – without speaking to him...

AVOID OVERSHADOWING

In the early stages of creating your interactive play experience, you need to be careful in your positioning so you are not imposing your presence on your dog. In particular, you must not overshadow him, as this can have a far-reaching effect on future interactions. Let me explain.

Let's think about a dog that has a great desire for his toy but does not, as yet, see the toy as part of an interactive experience with his handler. In this situation, if you use imposing body language or overshadow him, you give the impression that you are going to take away the toy.

Understandably, the dog reacts by trying to get away from you and starts to feel increasingly possessive over the toy. Confronted with the same scenario, a nervous dog is likely to let go of the toy, and will probably lose interest in the toy and the play experience altogether.

Students attending my seminars and workshops often wonder why our body language has such a massive effect on dogs when we share so much time together establishing a loving and affectionate bond.

I agree the concept may seem a little strange but, believe me, I have seen countless examples of how imposing body language and overshadowing can have a negative affect on creating interactive play experiences. Why is that?

ACTIONS AND ASSOCIATIONS

Take the example of a parent who gives a young child his or her favourite sweets, but as the child starts enjoying their treat, the parent takes it away with no explanation and nothing to replace it.

A nervous dog, or one that is unused to interactive play, may be intimidated if the handler bends over him.

But if you adopt an unimposing posture, your dog will grow in confidence.

As confidences increases, so comes the desire to interact with you.

Interactive play guide | 33

If this was repeated more than once, how long would it take for the child to realise that a treat that is freely given can just as easily be taken away? If this was repeated a handful of times, the child might well move away if the parent approached to hug or show affection, such is the strength of their association with their parent's previous behaviour. Would the child's reaction change if the parent explained that their approach meant a hug, or perhaps another sweet, was on offer?

Hopefully this scenario between a parent and child is unlikely to occur because it is simply unfair to withdraw a treat without good reason or some form of explanation. As fellow humans we can talk to each other and explain the reason for our actions, thus avoiding wrong associations which lead to all sorts of misunderstandings.

With this in mind, reflect on the dog who has leant that his favourite toy can be taken away from him at any time, but often the action is combined with imposing body language. This may be unintentional but it is easy to see why a dog makes an association between imposing body language and losing his toy, and reacts accordingly. We are not able to explain that our intention is to share the toy. In this case, our non-verbal communication really does speak louder than words.

IS YOUR DOG COMFORTABLE?

I often work with dogs that are uncomfortable with their handler's body language or positioning during play sessions. The dog that is worried by this form of non-verbal communication may display the following behaviour:

- Letting go of the toy as soon as the handler takes hold of it.
- Trying to drag the toy away from the handler and attempting to run away with his prize if he is allowed to win.

- Excessive or sporadic growling during interaction.
- Adjusting body position so as he is as far away from the handler as possible while still holding the toy in his mouth. The dog will often position his body at an angle.
- Complete disengagement from the handler and play experience, often opting to become consumed in a type of avoidance behaviour such as sniffing, chewing grass or urinating.

These are just a few examples of behaviour that a dog may show when he is concerned by his handler's body language during play.

Every dog is different and will non-verbally communicate their feelings in their own way. It will often be apparent when the dog becomes uncomfortable, as you will experience a problem that will affect the progression of your play development. Recognising whether your dog is comfortably engaged, or not, is vital as you are aiming to create a mutually enjoyable, beneficial and amazing interactive play experience.

WHAT TYPE OF BODY POSITIONING TO ADOPT DURING PLAY?

This is a great question and to avoid possible confusion, I have some very simple advice that I implement during play. Firstly, try to adjust your body position so that when you are interacting with your dog, you are leaning back slightly from the hand or hands that are holding the toy while the dog is engaged. Say to yourself: "avoid overshadowing", which is a simple way to remember that you must not overshadow your dog during play. It sounds like obvious advice but it is easy to form the unintentional habit of overshadowing your dog through your body positioning when you are playing.

A dog that is overawed by the play experience will find ways of disengaging...

36 | Interactive play guide

A CONSCIOUS CONSIDERATION

When you are playing with your dog, consider what effect your body language could be having on the result that you are achieving. If you make a conscious decision to do this at every play session, it is surprising how quickly it can become a really beneficial, unconscious skill. As a handler, you are used to the behaviour traits of your own dog and will adjust and adapt your body language organically, to suit him.

When it comes to your own dog, you are prepared to accept some of the problems that arise in play sessions and put them down to his individual behaviour quirks which cannot be resolved. However, I have seen how tiny adjustments in body language can alter the dynamics of an interactive play experience, often with very quick, highly positive results.

If you apply the techniques outlined in this book, your dog's desire for an interactive play experience will grow. In time, he may become desensitised to slight body language changes, but keeping a close check on your body language and positioning will always prove beneficial.

ACTING AND ANIMATION

Are you wondering what acting has got to do with interactive play skills? When I discuss acting and animation, I am not referring to what you might witness in a West End show. Well, not quite...If you are using body language and movement as a form of non-verbal communication to produce desired results when interacting with your dog, you must ensure that your intentions are animated and acted out to the extent that the information you are conveying is clear and easy to understand.

Let me give you some examples. In the previous chapter I explained how to interact with your dog for invincibility by playing an even tug of war. If you are working with a dog that doesn't have a great desire to play, he will need his confidence building in the tugging department so he is made to feel invincible. So, when he tugs on his toy, no matter how delicately, you need to boost his confidence and his feeling of invincibility by acting as though he is dragging you along and is far superseding your own strength. To make the dog truly believe he is capable of this feat, you must employ sufficient acting skills to show him, via non-verbal communication, that his efforts are paying off.

Another example of when acting and animation is required is when you are encouraging your dog to come back to you after he has won his toy. This can be challenging, particularly if your

Play a part so your dog buys into the game.

dog is possessive with the toy and likes to keep it to himself. In this situation I have seen many handlers freeze. Typically the handler will call the dog repeatedly, with perhaps a clap of the hands and a shuffle of their feet, too often to no avail.

In many cases the dog has become completely desensitised to the handler's voice – and to his own name – in a situation that has been repeated many times. Generally, the end result is the dog rewards himself by having a fantastic time with his toy on his own. To resolve this situation you have got to become animated, using your energy, movement and body language, to encourage the dog to come back to you. You have got to make yourself so interesting that the dog cannot help but return to you. How can you do this?

This is the time to use unconventional, exciting and inviting movements and body language. Moving towards the dog will encourage even the most unpossessive individual to move in the opposite direction, so you need to move backwards, away from the dog, working in an unconventional format such as zig zagging.

Your animation technique will have to be adjusted and adapted to suit your dog's needs, but that being said, a little shuffle of the feet and modest hand clapping is seldom enough to communicate that all the fun is with the handler.

Becoming animated, exciting and inviting, coupled with the enjoyment the dog has just experienced during your interaction, makes it far more likely that he will return to reinitiate the game. This is why acting and animation skills are irreplaceable when creating interactive play experiences. They are a valuable component in your non-verbal communication tool kit; failure to employ them can often be the reason behind poor outcomes and a lack of results.

SQUARING UP

The natural stance for a handler is to face a dog square on when interacting with him. Once you have created an interactive play experience, most dogs will be perfectly happy with this body positioning. However, the problem arises when starting out with a dog that may be nervous or toy possessive. Facing the dog head-on makes overshadowing an easy trap to fall into, as a handler will naturally lean over the dog to brace him/herself when tugging on the toy. I have achieved much success with adjusting my body position so that during interaction the dog is to the side of my body or even just behind me.

This may sound a bit odd, but it vastly decreases the likelihood of leaning over the dog, as bending sideways or backwards is a much more uncomfortable than bending forwards. These body positions are also far less imposing than standing head-on as they break the silhouette of your body and form a less daunting picture.

TO STAND OR NOT TO STAND?

This is a question that is worth considering during your interactive play sessions. When training or interacting with your dog, you spend much of the time standing up. So it is natural that when you consider interacting with your dog during play, your instinct is to stand. But in doing this, it is very easy to overshadow him.

Is there another way?

During interactive sessions, I very often take to the ground, crouching down or taking up a commando crawling type position depending on the dog that I am working with. I often use these lowered body positions with new dogs, but also with dogs that I have been working with for some time.

If you allow the dog to be positioned to the side of your body, rather than directly in front, you will not appear so imposing.

I have discovered that adjusting my body position, so that I am on a more equal level with the dog, will produce amazing results, boosting both confidence and energy levels during the interaction.

These lowered body positions eradicate the risk of overshadowing, and make the acting and animation involved in the even tug of war even more effective than when the handler is standing. Being lower to the ground also has great benefits when interacting with your dog in the even tug war, described in the previous chapter. When your dog tugs on his toy and you go with its force, effectively crawling in the direction that the dog is pulling, you will see his confidence, energy and motivation build as he rapidly makes the association that this really *is* an even tug of war.

By adopting a similar body position, you do not appear imposing, enhancing his belief that this is an even interaction, conducted on a level playing field. This is not to say that you should be rolling around on the floor every time you interact with your dog. But if you maintain a lowered body position in the early stages of interactive play, your dog's confidence, energy and motivation levels elevate at a faster rate, allowing you to gradually work your way to a normal standing position with your dog showing the same elevated desire level as when you were crawling.

When adjusting from a commando crawling position to a standing posture, progress in incremental steps, adopting several different positions, each slightly closer to the end goal of standing up. For example, commando crawl to a doggy

In some situations, much benefit can be accrued from adopting a lowered body position

crawl position to a kneeling position to a squatting position to a crouched position to standing. If you advance too quickly, it could come as a shock to your dog and may have an undesirable effect.

EYE CONTACT

The subject of eye contact goes hand in hand with your body language and positioning, and is equally important. The effects that intense or prolonged eye contact can have on a dog during interactive play can be counter-productive and block positive development. Obviously you are going to make eye contact with your dog during interactive play at some point – after all, you will be observing his body language and behaviour. Fleeting eye contact is unavoidable, but I would highly recommend you make the conscious effort to avoid intense, intentional or prolonged eye contact during play sessions. After working with many different dogs in many different spheres, I have experienced the detrimental effects that eye contact can have on dogs and it is because of this I suggest that we keep it to a conscious minimum during play.

TOO CLOSE FOR COMFORT

I often work with dogs that feel very uncomfortable when they are too close to their handler during play sessions; some even refuse to hold on to the toy when their handler is close enough to interact with them. This type of dog will be happy to run around, holding the toy, when he can please himself, but he will keep a distance from his handler to avoid interaction. If he does get close, he will either drop the toy as soon the handler tries to take hold of it to interact, or he will show some of the uncomfortable behaviour traits discussed earlier (see: Is your dog feeling comfortable? page 34).

If your dog is showing signs of concern, it is not advisable to force the issue by coming in close to initiate interactive play. Far from achieving the desired result of overcoming the problem, it can often cause conflict issues.

Equally you don't want to engage in an unproductive game of cat and mouse – trying to move in on your dog when he is trying to get away – as this will have negative effects on creating your interactive play experience.

The best strategy is to make use of a light line and a soft flat collar during play (see Proud parade process, page 17) as this is hugely relevant if your dog likes to keep his toy to himself, and does not want to come close to his handler. As with so many facets of dog training, this has to be a gradual process. In this situation, I use a light line and attach the dog's favourite toy or, alternatively, I work with a manufactured toy that already has a line attached.

This training aid can be used in a number of scenarios, discussed later in this book, but in this instance, you can place yourself at a distance but still allow the dog to interact with the toy, and therefore with you.

Essentially the light line becomes a toy extension; using this method you can now follow the steps covered in the previous chapter, Interaction For Invincibility, and begin the even tug of war interaction from a distance that is within your dog's comfort zone.

The toy extension is part of a process; if this method is applied over time you will be able to gradually work your way closer to your dog during interactive play. As he becomes increasingly receptive to your non-verbal communication, his desire for interactive play will develop and he will slowly lose the negative association with close-up interaction. Eventually you will be

Eye contact may be favoured by people when they communicate but it can have a detrimental effect on a dog.

Some dogs get worried if the handler is too close for comfort.

This is easily resolved by creating distance. Note the happy, relaxed body posture of this youngster.

able to replace the light line with a shorter line or, as in many cases that I have helped with, you will be able to get rid of the line altogether.

It is important to remember that fading out the line is an incremental process that should relate to the development of your interactive experience. Try not to rush, as you want your dog to comfortably engage with you and enjoy the experience. How can you determine how quickly – or slowly – you should progress from distance play to moving in close? In fact, your dog will dictate the pace. He will be taking on board your non-verbal communication and you will see subtle changes in his behaviour which will indicate how he is feeling.

Throughout the process you must remember to maintain an unimposing position so you are sending out a positive message. If you keep a close check on your dog, never moving closer until he 'tells you' he is comfortable, he will cease to worry about your proximity. By the time you have faded out the toy extension, he should be just as comfortable playing close up as he was when you were interacting at a distance. Through this process, the dog's desire for interactive play will develop, and as a consequence you will see notable improvements in his behaviour and body language. The perfect scenario is for the dog to be so comfortable that when he interacts with his handler close up and is allowed to win the toy, he comes straight back to continue interactive fun.

The time involved in achieving this goal will depend on the dog that you are working with. The most important thing to remember is not to rush the process, as lasting results will only be achieved by moving at a pace that your dog is comfortable with. Take small steps for lasting, positive and beneficial change.

CONTACT WITH YOUR DOG

The use of contact or touch during interactive play is another, irreplaceable form of non-verbal communication. I fully believe that it is the cornerstone of the interactive play experience, and when handlers are struggling, it is lack of contact that proves to be the missing link

Sharing affection with your dog, via physical contact, whether it is smoothing, stroking or even cuddling, is something that most handlers do on a daily basis. For a high percentage of dogs, this way of sharing affection has a positive association and is something that both handler and dog enjoy. Think of your own dog. Does he find physical contact rewarding? The answer to this question is probably "yes", so why do so many of us fail to utilise this valuable asset during our play experience? For many the reason is subconscious; the handler is so busy focusing on the toy, making physical contact with the dog rarely crosses their mind. Physical contact has multiple functions: it can be used to share affection, to stimulate a dog during interactive play, or to calm him. However, the way that the physical contact is delivered is important and, as with every aspect of developing the interactive play experience, it has to be tailored to suit a dog's individual needs.

Firstly, let us look at the delivery of touch. You already have superior knowledge on this subject as you know what your dog likes best. You will have discovered where and how he likes to be touched. It will be therefore be beneficial to utilise this knowledge by only smoothing or stroking him in these areas, making sure you avoid more sensitive places.

Most of all when delivering touch, you need to be completely considerate of your dog's needs. Try not to deliver your touch by simply lowering a flat hand over the dog's head from above.

Instead, make contact with the hand that is not holding the toy, allowing it to flow in rhythmically, from unimposing angles, so that your dog barely notices the delivery of the touch. Do not be fooled by this, the contact is having a very beneficial effect.

But how can you capitalise on physical contact in your interactive play experience? I use contact for three main purposes: sharing affection, restoring calm and as a means of providing positive stimulation. Each application serves a different purpose but all are closely linked; the two commonalities are that they are all a form of sharing affection and that the handler is always the distributor.

SHARING AFFECTION

Using physical contact to share affection serves as a great method of positive reinforcement and is a valuable asset when building the relationship necessary for your interactive play experience to thrive.

How to share? I would like you to take a moment to consider your dog's favourite form of physical affection that you give, not when you are playing but in a completely relaxed environment, whether that is in the living room in the evening or in the kitchen, first thing in the morning or last thing at night.

For example, my old dog likes to be scratched just behind his ear, some dogs enjoy having their hindquarters rubbed, others prefer being smoothed from their head and down their back.

Work out what is best for your dog, and implement it from unimposing angles so that your touch flows rhythmically into your interactive play experience. The dog should scarcely notice the delivery of the touch; he should simply enjoy the effect. This form of touch already has a positive association for your dog. When used during play, it helps to solidify the foundations of your relationship and produces super results. Another common reason why affection is rarely shared during play is because of the dog's reaction to the handler's hands getting too close to the toy. He associates this with having the toy taken away, which is a very natural response for even the most un-possessive dog.

How does sharing affection help to overcome this association? By using physical contact to share affection, and as a source of positive reinforcement, you are effectively breaking the old association and creating a new one. You will notice that after a time, your dog will see your hands approaching and he will associate this with an offer of affection rather than being the means of losing his toy.

This new association will prove to be far more beneficial and congruent for your interactive play and for your relationship. As with all good things, we do not over-use the sharing of affection. Just as with all aspects of your interactive play development, it needs to be in balance and customised to suit your dog. If you are working with a dog that has very little desire to play but is very people orientated, affection sharing via physical contact should only be given in small doses to begin with.

This is because the physical contact could result in the dog letting go of the toy, in preference for pure affection – in other words, a cuddle. As the dog's desire to play builds, you can slowly increase the contact, as the affection will become part of your interactive play experience.

On the other hand, if I was working with a dog that was possessive of his toy, and was not accustomed to affection sharing during interactive play, I would use the little and often approach to introduce the dog to the benefits of affection. In all situations, the way you share affection needs to be customised to suit your dog. Once you have found the right balance, it will serve as an irreplaceable part of your interactive play process.

CALMING CONTACT

Physical contact can also be used to calm your dog during interactive play. Why is this necessary? If you refer back to the previous chapter (Sharing the moment, page 18), you will see that a pause – a quiet moment to enjoy the experience – is an essential aspect of interactive play.

Creating calmness will also serve you well if you are working with a dog that is overly erratic in his behaviour during play interaction. A pause in proceedings will teach him that just because the toy isn't activated, it doesn't mean it will be taken away. Instead the handler shares a calm moment of affection with the dog, which really helps to reduce toy possession issues.

What is calming contact? In essence calming contact is another form of sharing affection, but in this instance you are intentionally delivering the touch to produce a calming effect.

When you are sharing affection with your dog via physical contact, the natural tendency is to up the pace, increasing speed and intensity, which leads to excitability. In contrast, when you are sharing affection to produce a calming effect, your physical contact needs to be calm, rhythmical and slower than your conventional method of giving affection.

Try using the flat of your hand to smooth the dog in a back and forth motion in an area of his body that feels comfortable for him. This very often produces a calming effect. In fact, I have found that the the most effective way to produce a calming effect is to share affection in your accustomed manner, but to use a slower and calmer delivery. For example, if you are sharing the moment with your dog while he is next to you, holding the toy in his mouth, you can calmly share affection by smoothing the top of his head from front to back with the flat of your hand in a very slow, rhythmical motion. This leads to

Smoothing can have a very calming effect.

the dog becoming less erratic and far calmer, and ready for the next session of interactive play. When you are giving physical contact to produce calmness, you will need to make a conscious effort to remember the points mentioned above, as the way you deliver will make all the difference.

POSITIVE STIMULATION

With a dog that is very comfortable with his handler and clearly enjoys physical contact during play, you can implement physical contact as a method of providing positive stimulation during the interactive play experience. This type of contact is usually of a higher tempo and a little more energetic than when used to produce calmness or when simply sharing affection.

It often produces a heightened performance from the dog so it should only be used with dogs that are very comfortable with their handlers, and with physical contact. How to provide stimulation? This is another form of sharing affection so you can call on your superior knowledge as to what type of physical contact stimulates your dog generally. Take a moment to think about how you would use physical contact at home to get your dog excited and to engage in play. More often than not it will

It is obvious that this dog is very relaxed and enjoys physical contact that is at a higher intensity.

be similar to the way you share affection, but delivered with a higher degree of energy and intensity. If your dog thrives on the type of physical contact, use it as a means to provide positive stimulation, which will produce a more interactive and energetic play experience.

FINAL THOUGHT ON PHYSICAL CONTACT

So often it seems that when we play with our dogs, our attention is entirely focused on the stimulation – or lack of stimulation – derived from the toy. But for the play experience to become truly interactive, we need be the creator of an amazing experience. Implementing physical contact, as described, into your interactive play experience can often prove to be the missing link.

MOVEMENT

When you play with your dog, you move your body – and movement is a huge part of the interactive play experience. The way you move is another way of communicating non-verbally with your dog and will therefore have a big impact. The question is: what type of movement works best?

DANCE WITH YOUR DOG!

I often compare the movement and rhythm involved in effective interactive play with dancing. The aim is to incorporate all of the movements discussed in this book, add a little rhythm, and create an interactive play dance. Typically I would place the body movements, or dancing, that I see during play sessions into two categories.

Firstly, there is a type of break dancing with lots of erratic, unpredictable, high tempo movements; the second has a measured pace with very slow movements that are rhythmical but repetitive.

Both of these dances have their pros and cons. The erratic movements of break dancing can have negative effects on your dog's development during interaction, but the energy involved is certainly useful when it comes to interactive play. The smoothness of movement involved in a slow dance can be really beneficial during your play sessions, but the range and type of movement may not be sufficient to stimulate and engage your dog. The type of dance you use will be dependant on your dog and what works best for him.

You will be able to slightly adjust and adapt the techniques outlined in this book to create your own dance. I have helped to create many interactive play dances and I have found that the most success lies in the middle ground, somewhere between break dancing and slow dancing – and I call it...

THE CANINE CHA CHA

I named this dance the canine cha cha because it is easy to remember – and it makes me smile every time I say it! The canine cha cha needs all the energy and motivation that is involved in high tempo break dancing, but it has all the smoothness and rhythm of a slow dance. I bet you never thought that you would be considering learning a new dance when you started reading this book? Well, here goes...

CUSTOMISED CHOREOGRAPHY

All of the techniques and movements discussed in this book will serve as the foundation for forming your own customised canine cha cha. It is then a case of adjusting and adapting your techniques, movements and body language so that your dog is comfortable and motivated during your dance.

Again, you have a huge advantage when it comes to developing your dance as you are already aware of the movement and body language that motivates your dog and, equally, the movement

Throw your inhibitions away and dance with your dog!

and body language that he finds uncomfortable. Once this is established, you need to add a healthy portion of rhythm and calculate the speed that will best suit your dog. You will soon find what works for your dog – and what will produce the best results. The only way to perfect your customised canine cha cha is by practising, adjusting and adapting your techniques to suit you and your dog.

By being considerate, and following the advice in this book, you will be able to choreograph a dance that is ideally suited to your dog. This may not always go exactly to plan, so it is important not to lose heart and remember that having fun is what interactive play is all about.

If you make sure that your dog always finishes the session with a positive play-related outcome, the practice will pay off. In no time you will learn how to fine tune and tweak your dance so you move in harmony with your dog, and you both start having fun with it. As your interactive play experience develops so will your dance; soon it will become an unconscious but really enjoyable part of your interactive play experience.

LAST THOUGHTS ON NON-VERBAL COMMUNICATION

When I am working with dogs, my priority is to find the easiest way to articulate my intentions or purpose to an animal that does not share the same language. Through experience and practice, the forms of non-verbal communication outlined in this chapter have proved irreplaceable to me and, if used correctly, they will serve you extremely well as you create your own interactive play experience.

TOY SELECTION

There is a vast range of toys on the market, so choosing something suitable for your dog should be pretty simple. However, if you give it a little extra thought, it will often prove hugely beneficial and make all the difference to your interactive play experience.

Some dogs just love toys and will play with anything; I have worked with countless service and sporting dogs that will happily play and interact with something as seemingly uninteresting as a small piece of garden hose.

You could be forgiven for thinking that there is no need to waste time thinking about toy selection for this type of dog – after all, he will play with anything. But if you want to get the most from interactive play, you will find that the better suited the toy is to your dog, the better your play experience will be.

In contrast, you may have a dog that is simply not interested in toys of any type. If this is the case, you will need to think a little differently about which toy you choose, and often this involves thinking outside the toy box. In the course of my work, I was contacted by a woman who was completely convinced that no toy existed that her dog would play with.

After some investigative questions on my part I discovered that the only article the dog showed interest in was his bedding. Much to the owner's dismay, it had to be replaced on a regular basis as her little dog would often destroy it.

You need to work out what toy motivates your dog – and suits his physical make-up.

Interactive play guide | 59

Can you guess what's coming next? I suggested that she exchanged her dog's bedding for something equally as comfortable but made from different material, and brought the bedding along to our forthcoming appointment.

When we met, I cut a small piece of bedding from the whole, and activated it just as I would a normal toy. In a very short time, the dog had engaged and was playing interactively, albeit with a chewed bit of bedding and a stranger. It was easy to transfer the interaction to the owner, and after building on this, she was able to sew the bedding into a tug toy shape. To this day, she still uses the bedding as her play toy and is able to enjoy her interactive play experiences to the full.

This is a good example of how thinking a little bit differently about your choice of interactive play toy can have a big effect on the outcome. In this case the toy selection solved solve two problems as the little dog also stopped destroying his bedding... result! Selecting a toy that suits your dog can play a big part. it is so easy to go for a toy that looks amazing, but it may not necessarily be the best match for your dog. Your dog may engage with it, but it may mean that your interactive play still does not reach its potential.

MAKING THE CHOICE

How do you choose a toy that suits your dog? There are a number of factors to consider:

MOUTH SHAPE

The shape of your dog's mouth will very often determine the shape or type of toy that is most suitable. If the toy fits comfortably into your dog's mouth, he will find it much easier to take a firm grip during interactive play.

For example, if I am interacting with a dog that has shorter,

You may have to experiment to find a toy that your dog truly values.

more rounded mouth, such as a Boxer, a softer ball on a rope is a good fit. On the other hand, if I am working with a dog with a longer more pointed mouth, such as a Belgian Malinois, a wider and flatter tug toy works well.

When you choose a toy that suits your dog's mouth shape and fills his mouth comfortably, it helps to reduce mouthing and chomping down on the toy, and encourages a firm grip. Have you ever watched a dog playing with a tennis ball, particularly when the tennis ball is too small and incorrectly shaped for the dog's mouth shape?

The dog will often mouth, chomp and even chew the tennis ball until he destroys it. This is his reaction to being given something that does not fit comfortably in his mouth, and shows the detrimental effect of providing the 'wrong' toy. Establishing a firm grip is key to interactive play, and if you choose a toy that allows this, you are one step closer to establishing a positive, interactive experience.

TOY SIZE

The size of the toy you select can also have an effect on your dog's willingness to engage. How could selecting a toy that is too small for your dog affect your interactive play experience? Firstly and most importantly, there is the safety factor; a toy that is small enough to become lodged in a dog's throat must be avoided at all costs. But there are other issues to consider in terms of the play experience. If the toy leaves nothing for the handler to get hold of when it is in the dog's mouth, it is very difficult to take part in the interaction for invincibility (see Chapter One).

For example have you ever tried to interact in an even tug of war, with your dog, using a standard tennis ball? Not only is it virtually impossible to engage, it can also cause long term problems as repeating this awkward interaction can lead to possessiveness of the toy and disinterest in the interactive experience. This can start in a very subtle way: the dog may twist his head to one side when the handler reaches for the tennis ball. A small sign of avoidance, but it is significant. If a little more thought is given to toy selection, the problem will not arise.

What happens if you choose a toy that is too big for your dog? Some dogs are happy to interact with an over-sized toy and will experience no problems whatsoever. If your dog's favourite toy is over-sized and causing no issues, stick with it.

The size of the toy must work for you, and your dog.

As I emphasise throughout this book, we must adjust and adapt our methods to suit our dogs. However, many dogs struggle to cope with a toy that is too big. Typically, a dog that is playing with an over-sized toy will repeatedly try to readjust his grip as he is unable to get a firm hold on the toy. Imagine taking a child to a large playground with lots of fun apparatus. The child is so excited, he/she wants to play on everything, all at the same time. But after a while, the child finds their favourite, which offers the most enjoyment, and so plays on that piece of equipment until exhausted.

A similar sense of excitement often causes a dog to keep readjusting on an over-sized toy, which then becomes habitual during play. This can lead to the dog consistently chewing and ultimately destroying toys whenever the opportunity arises.

As already highlighted you need find a toy that fits your dog's muzzle shape, but you need to be able to take a hold of the toy comfortably so you can interact with him. Therefore, if your dog is best suited to interacting with a ball, opt for a ball on a rope which offers plenty of holding space for the handler. If your dog prefers a tug toy, choose a two-handled version which allows easy interaction between dog and handler.

What should you do if your dog's favourite toy has nothing for you to hold on to? For example, he may want to play with a knotted rope toy, or you may be making use of an article he likes, such as the piece of bedding mentioned earlier. In this situation you need to keep a close correlation between the size of the toy and the shape of your dog's muzzle in terms of width and length.

The toy needs to be of sufficient length so the dog can get a mouthful, and the handler can hold it with both hands. Ideally, the dog grips the toy in the centre and the handler holds it with one hand either side of the dog's mouth. As a point of reference,

I would suggest that the toy's length equals the width of the dog's mouth, plus three hand-widths.

You will often find that once you have found a toy that is sized and shaped to suit your dog, his attempts to readjust his grip will reduce. Your dog will soon discover that one mouthful of his favourite toy, coupled with your interaction, is far more enjoyable than trying to get ten mouthfuls at once. Establishing a firm grip is an important part of the interactive play experience, and if your dog is consistently readjusting or attempting to destroy his toy, it will make your experience unnecessarily difficult. Keep these tips on size and shape in mind when selecting a toy and I can guarantee it will make all of the difference.

WHAT IS YOUR TOY MADE OF?

The material that your toy is made of can have an effect on creating your interactive play experience. Why is that? Just as it is beneficial to consider the size and shape of your toy, it can be hugely beneficial to consider the material that your toy is made of. Unlike the size and shape of your toy, where we can use the structure and size of our dog's mouth to help us in our selection, the choice of the material boils down to what your dog is comfortable with. Some dogs are naturally a little harder mouthed than others. A German Shepherd is often suited to a tougher more resilient material, like a tug toy made of a fire hose type material.

On the other hand, if you have a soft-mouthed dog, such as a Cocker Spaniel, you may experience more success with a correctly-sized foam ball on a rope. There are many exceptions to these examples: I have worked with Cockers who like tough-textured tuggies and Shepherds who prefer soft, squidgy toys – it is all about discovering what suits your individual dog. How do you know what material is correct for your dog? If you have followed the advice on size and shape of the toy, given in this chapter, and you are still experiencing problems with excessive mouthing, lack of desire to keep grip or general lack of interest in the toy, the material of the toy could be the key.

Allow me to refer to my trusted friend the tennis ball for another example. I would like to stress at this point that I am not against using tennis balls in interactive play – but they often highlight issues relating to the play experience. At a seminar I was giving, one of the students told me that he was struggling to play with his Cocker Spaniel with a rubber ball on a rope, as every time the dog engaged with the toy he would quickly adjust his grip and ultimately lose interest. I asked the student what happened if he used the same toy in a game of fetch? He explained that the dog would run out, pick up the toy, return with it and drop it at his feet several times over, and would then start returning without the toy.

He said it was the complete opposite when he played with a tennis ball; the dog kept a firm grip on it at all times, fetching the ball and only releasing it when asked. However, as discussed earlier, the tennis ball did not work for interactive games as the student had nothing to hold on to.

Evaluating the dog's behaviour with both the tennis ball and the rubber ball on a rope, it was clear that the rubber material was simply too hard for the dog. My solution to the problem was very simple: I suggested he drilled a hole though the tennis ball so he could thread a rope through it. This was one of my "here's one I made earlier" moments. I had a toy of this type to hand, and when we tried it, the success was pretty much instantaneous. The dog had made his preference abundantly clear and as soon as we listened to him, we got results.

The question is how do you go about finding a material that suits your dog? The best plan is to assemble a selection of

Find out if your dog is hard-mouthed or soft-mouthed – and then pick an appropriate toy.

Interactive play guide | 67

toys made from different materials, and then throw each one, in turn, for your dog to fetch. You are looking for the toy that he picks up with ease and holds without mouthing. It is then a case of either making a suitably sized and shaped toy out of that material, or choosing a toy that is a good match.

DOES YOUR DOG HAVE A FAVOURITE?

We have talked about the steps to take when selecting a new interactive play toy for your dog. But before you start seeking out, making or buying a brand new toy, you should first ask yourself whether your dog already has a favourite play article?

It may be that your dog already has a favourite toy.

I use the term 'play article' because you may already have the answer. If you are struggling to find a toy that motivates your dog, think about the old slipper he carries around the house, or the tea towel he steals from the kitchen counter. If your dog has a favourite article already, why not capitalise on this asset to stack the odds in your favour? As described earlier with the dog who loved his bedding, you can modify and customise the article so that it suits your dog and becomes your interactive play toy. Obviously you must ensure that when modifying articles, there is no potential risk to your dog.

CONSIDERING THE OPTIONS

I could fill a book of this size simply by listing the toy options that are available. If you want to take a look at what you can buy, spend a few minutes on your laptop or visit your local pet shop. In most cases, I find that the temptation is to choose a toy that is visually pleasing, rather than one that most suits the dog. However, you now have the tools (size, shape, material) to select an interactive play toy, or modify an article into an interactive toy so that it best suits your dog's needs. This will make the selection process much easier – and leave more time for interactive play!

ONCE YOU HAVE STRUCK GOLD

Let's look at something we regard as a treat – in this instance I will address the chocolate lovers among us. In most cases, chocolate is viewed as an occasional treat rather than something that is consumed all the time. The amount you choose to treat yourself is a matter of personal preference – and nobody is counting...

But it is because we enjoy chocolate on a treat basis that the experience is enhanced. If chocolate was the only food you were allowed to eat, how long would it take to loose its appeal? For the vast majority of us, it would not take long for chocolate to become less appealing. But more importantly, the feeling of enhanced enjoyment that was derived from eating chocolate would diminish due to over consumption and simply having too much of a good thing.

Bearing this in mind, when you strike gold and find your interactive play toy, I suggest that this toy is only used for your interactive play experience. If you dog has too much exposure to his toy, or has un-interactive access to it, he will gradually start to lose interest in it. The interactive toy should be something that you share with your dog as an exclusive part of your interactive play experience.

The toy you choose should be reserved exclusively for interactive play sessions.

This will help to maintain your dog's desire for the toy and will often enhance your interactive play experience – in just the same way as a human gets more enjoyment from eating chocolate as a treat. If the toy is produced only for interactive play, your dog will very soon begin to associate the toy with the pleasure of sharing the interactive play experience with you.

If your dog is allowed un-interactive access to the interactive toy, it can encourage bad habits. For example, if your dog has the toy in the house when he is on down time, he is highly likely to start chewing it, which, as we know, can hinder our interactive play experience.

Just as importantly, over exposure to the toy may result in the dog gradually losing interest in it. For your interactive toy to retain maximum value, only share it when it is a part of the amazing play experience that you have created.

TOY SELECTION REFLECTION

What is the ideal toy you would like to share with your dog for your interactive play process? Everybody's answer to this question is different. When I work with police officers or sporting handlers, a common response is they want to use a toy that will fit in a pocket so it can be produced for interactive play, and enjoyed as a reward during training.

On the other hand, when I visit pet clubs the toys that I see are pretty spectacular, in all shapes, sizes and colours. There is no right or wrong when it comes to choosing a toy. Everybody has their own ideas, but the overriding factor must be that it meets the needs of the individual dog. Watch your dog when he is playing, take on board the tips outlined in this chapter, and then you will come up with the perfect toy which will lead to a far better interactive play experience.

ENERGY'S EFFECTS

Energy is a really important part of creating your interactive play experience, but it is something that is often overlooked – so much so that I have decided to dedicate a whole chapter to the subject. You may well be wondering what I mean by energy?

To best understand the concept, I would like to divide it into two categories: mental energy and physical energy. Both types of energy are hugely relevant to both handler and dog, and for the whole play experience.

PROJECTING A MIND-SET

When you are working with a dog, it is not just a matter of what you say and do that influence his behaviour, he will also be responding to something much more subtle. In fact, it is so subtle, you may not even be aware of the vibes you are transmitting. To understand what is going on, I will look at the potential effects of both negative and positive energy.

DISBELIEVERS AND NEGATIVE MENTAL ENERGY

Can you think of a time when you were planning to train your dog to do something – a trick, or a new exercise – but for some reason you doubted that it would work? If you went ahead with the training session, it probably did not produce the result that you would have liked. Why is that? If the self-doubt was in your mind before you started your training session or occurred at any

Negative mental energy will make your dog a non-believer.

time during the session, the negative mental energy that you projected would have had a negative effect on your behaviour. This would almost certainly have been relayed to your dog, which, in turn, would have had a negative effect on his state of mind and behaviour. This negative mental energy, coupled with the behaviour changes it produces, has a detrimental effect on your own and your dog's performance, which often sets the tone for your training session. This negative energy then has a domino effect. Because of the negative mental energy, and the effect it has on yourself and your dog, the training fails to go according to plan.

As soon as this happens – even to the smallest degree – our brain cuts in, telling us: "you knew this wasn't going to work; I don't know why you are bothering". At this point we generally agree with our brain and stop what we are doing, often without producing any results and settling for the fact that we have failed in what we were trying to do. Negative mental energy can have an equally negative effect on your interactive play experience. It influences the way you and your dog perform as a team and you will achieve less than you are easily capable of.

Why does your mental energy have such an impact on your dog? It is because you and your dog are a team working together in unison, mentally and physically. How you think, and the effect this has on your behaviour, can directly affect your dog. You therefore need to dispel negative thoughts from your mind, regardless of whether you are training or playing with your dog, and become a believer, generating positive mental energy.

BELIEVERS AND POSITIVE MENTAL ENERGY

To succeed at anything that you undertake with your dog, you must first believe it is possible; creating your interactive play experience is no different.

When I talk to people about the effect that negative mental energy and belief can have, there are varied reactions. I can see that many think that if the technique is correct, the process should work. There is truth in this but if you do not believe in what you are doing, you will not reach your full potential and achieve the best possible results. Think about the training example that I gave at the beginning of this chapter where a negative mind-set led to negative results. Now let's turn the tables.

If, before that training session, you had decided that the way you were going to teach the exercise was perfectly suited to your dog and therefore success was guaranteed, there would have been a completely different outcome. The belief instilled in your mind would have produced and projected positive mental energy.

Positive mental energy makes you feel good and will have a positive effect on your behaviour and performance, which is transferred directly to your dog. The training plan was unlikely to fail because of the difference your mind-set and new positivity projection would have made to you and your dog's learning environment.

If a problem had arisen, a positive mind-set would have enabled you to adjust and adapt your techniques to suit your dog and get the best result possible.

Time and time again, I have seen how lack of belief and positive mental energy can have such a negative impact that the possibility of creating an amazing interactive play experience is lost. If you have taken on the belief that your dog will not play, it will become a reality because you will not put in the energy that is needed. Our minds are powerful things: belief and positive mental energy are crucial factors in achieving success.

CHANGING YOUR MIND-SET

How can you consciously change your mind-set? It is all well and good talking about it, but how can you switch your mind from doubt to belief? By reading this book and putting the information into action, you will be working in the most considerate and thoughtful way possible to develop you and your dog's interactive play experience.

You will be consciously adjusting and adapting your techniques so that all aspects of the experience are customised to suit your dog. This, in itself, will facilitate a shift in mind-set – often without your conscious realisation. By paying attention to detail, and understanding what your dog needs, you are laying the foundations for success, leaving nothing to chance or hope.

Get yourself into the right frame of mind before the work begins...

Negative mental energy is very often associated with doubt, which can lead to fear. Fear of what? Fear of it all going wrong; this fear generates negative mental energy, which is what we need to dispel.

Fear is much more likely to occur if you have given insufficient thought and preparation to the task ahead. If you have considered every aspect, and worked out how this is likely to affect your dog, you will become confident in what you are doing, and your mind-set will shift from doubt to belief. The domino effect will come into play in a positive way because you will experience some success with every interactive session, which will give you more and more confidence leading to a strong belief, consistent results and the creation of your amazing interactive play experience.

Before you begin a play session, take a few moments to remember that your interactive play process is something to be enjoyed – you are going to have fun. Close your eyes, take some deep breaths, which will begin to calm your mind, and think about all the enjoyment that you and your dog are going to have during your interactive play session. Visualise the process so you can imagine how good it is going to be.

This will ignite that amazing feeling that you are going to get when you are interacting with your dog before you have even begun. When you open your eyes you will be invigorated with belief, and in the best mind-set possible for your interactive play session.

You may think that this all sounds a bit silly but, believe me, it will pay back ten-fold in the form of positive mental energy during your play session. It is something that I do before every seminar, workshop or training session, and I advise all my clients to find time for a few moments' reflection before beginning the task ahead. Give it a try. Once you have done it and experienced the results, you won't look back. We have talked about the forces of negative and positive mental energy, and how you can consciously change your mind-set – but there is another factor to bear in mind when you are aiming to project positivity. It is important to *have fun* during your interactive play sessions: smile, laugh and enjoy the interaction with your dog.

This has proved to be the biggest generator of positive mental energy and will hugely benefit your play sessions. Using this information, and implementing it into your interactive play sessions, is another step on the path to success. Get started right away and feel and see the difference.

PHYSICAL ENERGY

By following your mental energy guide, you will be happy, invigorated, and in a positive state of mind, which tips the scales in your favour. This positive mental energy is required not only because it relays to your dog, it will also affect the amount of physical energy that you put into your interactive play sessions.

As we discussed in Chapter Two, you will be using non-verbal communication, articulating your intentions to your dog via your body language and movements. To do this effectively often requires physical energy, so lets talk about what to expect.

ENHANCING ENERGY AND EFFORT

Interactive play is an energetic activity which can be compared to a short work out. When your interactive play session is finished you should be a little out of breath, but feel invigorated with a sense of achievement.

You will be surprised at how good you feel! Just for the record, when I say a short work out I am not talking about gasping for breath or being drenched in sweat as if you had run a marathon.

It should feel more like the effects of going up a few flights of stairs, which leaves you feeling fresh and energised.

As you will have worked out by now, interactive play is an activity that is physically and mentally stimulating for both you and your dog.

To effectively share, enjoy and benefit from your interactive play experience, you have got to put as much effort into the session as your dog. In fact, at the beginning when you first start to create the experience, you may well have to put in more effort than your dog to develop his desire to engage.

Your success will be dependant on adjusting, adapting and applying the techniques that suit your dog, combined with the effort that you put into creating the play experience. Why is your physical energy a component part of the experience?

Can you think of a time when you prepared yourself to go to the gym, or to take part in a physical activity such as running? Now think of a similar experience, but this time you were given no prior warning.

If you compare the two experiences, you would almost certainly find that your exercise was far more productive when you had time to plan for it, rather than having it sprung upon you. Our minds and bodies always perform better when we prepare and know what's coming.

If you are planning a physical activity, it will not come as a shock when you do get a little out of breath. This is important because it is often at the point of becoming slightly out of breath that the inclination to stop creeps in. Unfortunately this can often lead to stopping an interactive play session just before the point that you and your dog get the best possible result.

However, when you are expecting a workout, you will continue a little longer. It may leave you feeling slightly out of breath, but it will almost certainly be accompanied by a feeling of achievement.

INCREASING YOUR ENERGY

By enjoying your interactive play sessions on a regular basis, you will naturally begin to adapt to the short workouts; that out of breath feeling will diminish until it eventually disappears.

This works in the exactly the same way as if you were visiting the gym on a regular basis, although as much as I love the treadmill, I'm pretty sure we can agree interactive play is far more enjoyable.

In time you will notice that your interactive play experience will organically supply you with more energy. This is because regular exercise is making you physically fitter, and this improved fitness will increase your energy production.

Regular sessions, where you practise the best-suited techniques, will see all areas of your interactive play experience develop and thrive – while you are having fun the whole time.

Experiencing this success will also have a beneficial effect on your energy levels. We have all experienced that physical 'high' that comes when we set a goal and achieve it. We thrive on success, and this feeling is often even more concentrated when you share the experience with your dog.

Regular practice, coupled with positive mental energy, will produce physical energy. The best thing is: you and your dog will love every step of the journey. So creating an interactive play experience has the dual effect of improving your physical fitness and energy levels, and enhancing your positive mental energy.

This change is most apparent to me when clients return after

If you feel fit, you will bring positive energy to your play sessions.

they have been working with their dogs for a few weeks. They often feel fitter; they are very positive about their new play experience and are producing amazing results with their dogs.

Both handler and dog are clearly benefitting, which affirms my long-held belief that interactive play is as good for you as it is for your dog. So that's you sorted. However, interactive play experience requires two to tango, so what about your dog's energy?

YOUR DOG'S ENERGY

Your dog's physical and mental energy also play a huge part in the positive development of your interactive play experience. It is both a physically and mentally stimulating activity, which exercises your dog's body and mind through interaction and stimulation.

Clients are often amazed at how tiring a short interactive play session proves to be for a dog. The mental and physical workout produces a contented dog who is happy to snooze on his bed for the remainder of the day.

As interactive play does use up a considerable amount of energy, the results that you experience often have a lot to do with your dog's energy levels.

Every dog's level will be unique to the individual, and it is likely that a large Mastiff will tire more quickly than a Border Collie. However, it is your job to get the best from your own dog's energy level, whatever that may be. The aim is to channel his energy productively rather than allowing him to waste energy by becoming distracted or offering behaviour that is not conducive to the interactive experience.

Can you think of a time when your dog's energy is at its peak – when he is having a mad five minutes? I'm sure most dog owners can relate to this. At this point the dog is pumped full of energy but has no idea what do with it, so he reverts to all sorts of strange, often hilarious activities.

Can you imagine the results if you could harness all that energy into an experience that you can share and enjoy with your dog?

You can – and I will show you how. But first we need to talk about confusion and energy.

CONFUSION BURNS UP ENERGY

Do you sometimes struggle to get your dog interested in his toy or in interacting with you? Or perhaps your dog loses interest in the interaction very quickly? These are common issues that I come across on a regular basis. Every dog is different, and because of this the causes can vary. However a state of confusion is often at the centre of the issue.

For example, you have planned an interactive play session with your dog about ten minutes from the outset of a walk, which is how long it takes to arrive at your preferred spot. So you clip on the lead, grab your toy and off you go.

You will probably be holding the toy so your dog can see it, and if you have hidden it, he will have a pretty good idea where it is. Understandably he is excited; he will be thinking :"I'm out on a walk and we are going to play, jackpot!" He doesn't know that you have a particular spot planned for your play session – he is ready to play right away.

He therefore burns up much of his energy anticipating the game, and by the time you reach your destination he has lost his desire to play, and is more interested in all of the wonderful smells and interesting things in the surrounding location.

This situation can be exacerbated depending on the handler's response to the dog's over-excited behaviour en route to the play destination. There are two common reactions. The handler may encourage the dog, geeing him up and teasing him with the toy.

Alternatively, the handler discourages the dog's excitement by reprimanding him. Both examples have a negative effect on the interactive play session ahead as the dog is frustrated in his desires at a time when he has maximum mental and physical energy. Teasing the dog and building anticipation will burn up energy at a rapid rate, leaving the dog uninterested in your interactive play session.

After all, he has just spent a good ten minutes trying to engage you in the experience, and he has got to the point when he no longer cares. Equally if you have attempted to curb his excitement and withdrawn the toy, he will not only have wasted energy feeling frustrated, he will also feel confused when you suddenly decide it is OK to play.

The examples given are slightly different but they have a similar outcome: a confused dog that has no idea when to play or when not to play, will use up a lot of his physical and mental energy.

OVERCOMING CONFUSION AND UTILISING YOUR DOG'S ENERGY

So how can we overcome the confusion? In fact, the answer is simple: you need to teach your dog a clear start and finish to your interactive play sessions. This can be compared to the principle of the school bell that most of us are familiar with.

The bell would ring at 9 am, and we had a clear understanding that this signalled the time to start class. We were also taught that when the bell rang again at 9.45 am, the class was finished. This is a very simple but super effective system of regulating behaviour, which is probably why it has lasted so long. I recommend that you choose a school bell of your choice.

I don't literally mean a school bell; my personal favourite type of 'school bell' is to use a play collar which makes simple work of teaching your dog the start and finish of interactive play sessions. This is how it works.

- Pick a familiar environment that your dog is comfortable with, which is safe and has enough room for an interactive play session. In most cases, your back garden works well.

- Put the toy and play collar in your pockets so that they will be hidden from your dog. Now you and your dog can make your way to the chosen interactive play area.

- Once in your play area, place the correctly fitted collar on your dog. You need to choose a collar that is different from his normal collar, preferably one that is extra soft and comfy and maybe a little wider.

- As soon as the collar is fitted, produce your toy and activate it to engage in your interactive play session.

- When it is time to end your play session, return the toy to your pocket and remove the play collar.

- Repeat this in the same environment on a daily basis over the course of a week. If you are consistent with using your collar in this way, your dog will soon associate the play collar with your interactive play sessions. The concept is simple: no collar no game, which your dog will understand very quickly.

- When you can see your dog is forming a good association between the collar and your play sessions, you can start to use the collar in the same way in different locations.

- The concept works best if the play collar is very different to

A play collar marks the beginning and end of a play session.

the one that your dog wears all of the time. Alternatively, a harness or even a word can be used as a cue to start and finish your play process.

Offering your dog a clear understanding of the start and finish of interactive play sessions can benefit your experience because it avoids confusion and capitalises on your dog's energy. You can teach your dog to understand exactly when you want to play so he applies maximum focus and energy – and you have the most fun possible during your play sessions.

IMPROVING AND MAXIMISING YOUR DOG'S ENERGY

We have now discussed utilising and focusing your dog's energy so that it is at its peak during your play sessions. Now let's talk about improving and maximising your dog's energy.

As with your own physical and mental energy, your dog's energy levels will improve with every interactive play session as his body and mind become accustomed to the experience.

Your dog will enjoy interactive play more and more with every session; he will be increasingly stimulated and will put in more effort. This increased output will have a beneficial effect on his physical and mental fitness, and his energy will be maximised during your play sessions. This is exactly the same as us working out on a treadmill; the more we work out, the more we enjoy the exercise.

As our enjoyment increases, we find ourselves pressing the resistance plus button, which leads to us becoming fitter. Regularly enjoying your play experience will begin to improve and maximise your dog's energy levels, paving the way for more interactive fun.

As your dog's desire for interactive play begins to elevate there are some other simple tips that will help to improve and maximise his physical and mental fitness.

Before we start on these tips, I would like to make a valuable suggestion. Before and after your interactive play sessions, or any other physical activity, I recommend at least five minutes of brisk lead walking, to warm up your dog's muscles prior to exercise, and to warm them down afterwards.

This will help to avoid injury and is good for the overall health of your dog – in exactly the same way, as we would warm up and warm down before and after sports activity at the gym.

A fit dog will be ready to buy into the game, and will be energised by your positive attitude.

MAXIMISING YOUR DOG'S PHYSICAL ENERGY

Interactive play is a short, relatively vigorous activity; this requires your dog to have a good sprint capability. We can work on improving this in two ways:

INTERACTIVE SPRINT FETCH INTERVALS

If your dog has a strong desire for his toy and, through your interactive play, is happy to bring it back to you and interact, I would suggest playing sprint fetch intervals over a short distance.

All you need is your dog, your interactive play toy and a safe, preferably grassed area to play.

- Ask your dog to sit by your side and throw your interactive play toy no further than 10 to 15 metres (30-50 ft).

- Wait until the toy has landed, then send your dog to fetch it. Asking your dog to wait until the toy has landed before you send him will avoid the injuries that occur with sliding and other acrobatics involved in diving after a moving toy.

- The next bit is really important: as your dog picks up his toy, call him once and then use non-verbal communication to encourage him back to you. As soon as he returns, interact with him for a short period in exactly the same way as in an interactive play session.

- Remember, we always want our dogs to see us as the creator of all of the best experiences in the world. If you do not interact with your dog when he returns to you, he could decide that the toy is more fun if he trots around the field with it in his mouth, rather than seeing it as part of your interactive play experience. This exercise will not only increase your dog's sprint capability but also improve his desire for the toy, both of which will help to improve your play.

INTERACTIVE SPRINT RECALLS

Maybe your dog is a little toy possessive, which is something you are working on while creating your play experience. You may be thinking that if you were to play interactive fetch with your dog, he may disappear to entertain himself with the toy at the first opportunity. If this is the case, interactive sprint recalls can work really well and offer a great alternative to interactive sprint fetch.

All you will need is your dog, your interactive play toy, a light training line to connect to your toy and a safe, preferably grassed, area to play in.

- Ask your dog to wait in a control position – a sit, down or stand – whichever he is most likely to hold. If you are not sure if you dog will wait in position, ask a friend wait with your dog. At this point, the toy, with the light training line connected to it, will be accessible but out of sight (in a jacket pocket, for example).

- Leave your dog in position and walk away from him; for the first time ten paces will be more than enough. Then stand, with your back to your dog, and get ready to produce the toy with the line attached. This will work best if you hold the toy in one hand and the end of the light line in the other.

- Now turn to face your dog. As soon as you are facing him, produce the toy and call your dog. When you produce the toy, it is important to hold it to one side away from your body, holding the end of the training line in the other hand.

- Your dog will come sprinting to you to fetch the toy from your hand. As he engages with the toy, let it go at the last moment while holding on to the end of training line. This reduces the impact on the dog and prevents him jolting himself when he engages the toy. Now take up the slack in the line and interact with your dog in exactly the same way as you would in your interactive play sessions.

- This exercise not only works on your dog's sprint capabilities, it also helps to affirm your recall. If your dog has no possession issues with his toy, you can carry out this exercise without a training line attached. Just be sure that the toy is held away from your body, and let go as the dog engages, to avoid impact. You can then call him once, and use your non-verbal communication to encourage him to come back to you and interact, so that, once again, you are the main source of interactive pleasure.

INTERACTIVE SEARCH AND RETRIEVE

Both of the previous exercises are focused primarily on improving and maximising your dog's physical energy through fitness and interaction.

You can also work to improve and maximise your dog's mental energy, and interactive search and retrieve is a great way of doing this. All that you need is your dog, your interactive play toy, and a safe search area where you can hide the toy.

A long light training line can also be used if your dog is a little toy possessive. In terms of a suitable search area you can use your garden, or a space in the local park, with slightly overgrown grass, works well.

You can also take the toy indoors and work in a garage, using old cardboard boxes to hide your toy.

- You can either ask your dog to wait by your side and throw the

You can build up your dog's desire for the toy by playing a game of interactive search and retrieve.

92 | Interactive play guide

toy into the search area, or he can wait alone (perhaps with a friend) while you hide the toy in the search area.

- If you choose to go into the search area to hide the toy, you need to make it really simple in the early stages by choosing an easy location so you can set him up for success. Once you have hidden the toy, make it clear that you no longer have the toy in your possession, then return to your dog's side. Now send him into the search area to find his toy. As your dog starts to understand this game, you can increase the degree of difficulty by making several pretend drops of the toy, and then leaving it in a hiding place.

- If you ask your dog to sit by your side while you throw the toy into the search area, he will become very skilled at pin-pointing where the toy has landed and the exercise will become more of a retrieve than a retrieve and search. So as he develops an understanding of the game, you can both turn a circle before sending him to find the toy.

- As he picks it up, up call him once and then use your non-verbal communication to encourage him to come back to you. As soon as he returns, interact with him for a short period.

- If your dog is a little toy possessive, attach a long light training line to a flat collar or harness so he cannot run away with his toy and entertain himself. This is an excellent exercise that will help to improve and maximise your dog's mental energy through the mental stimulation of searching for his toy and interacting with you.

The number of times you repeat any of these exercises is dependant on your dog's energy levels; the most important thing is to stop before he loses interest. The exercises are designed to help to improve and maximise your dog's energy, and every session should finish with him wanting more.

MOUNT ENERGY

During your interactive play sessions, or any of your energy maximising sessions, you need to think about Mount Energy.

Think of your interactive play sessions as climbing Mount Energy, beginning your session at the base of the mountain when your dog has maximum energy. So you begin climbing and, as the rhythm of the session settles, your dog's performance will improve.

You are likely to experience the best results about three-quarters of the way up the mountain, which is when your dog's energy levels are good and the effort he is putting into the interactive play experience is at its maximum. This is the best time to stop, leaving you dog still engaged and wanting more of the experience.

It is tempting to keep going to reach the peak of the mountain, but this can often be a mistake. If you try to reach the peak before your dog is ready, it can cause his energy level to drop, sometimes quite suddenly. The result will be that you finish the session with your dog disengaged and uninterested in the activity, which is effectively falling off the mountain and going back to the bottom.

It is far better to finish on a really positive note three-quarters of the way up. In this way you can allow your dog to recharge for an even better experience at the next session.

Facing page: Finish a play session before your dog begins to tire.

Interactive play guide | 95

RELATIONSHIP BUILDING

As I am sure you already know, there is something very special about sharing a good relationship with your dog.

We love all of the amazing elements – my personal favourite is being greeted with absolute delight, even when I have only been gone for two minutes.

We also accept the parts that we are not so fond of, such as the times when your dog completely ignores you when he is in the company of other dogs, or when he pulls like a sled dog when he is on the lead. We embrace the good, and the not so be good, because of the strength of our relationship.

We can also be passive in our relationship, accepting how things are rather than trying to change or improve them. There is a missing link in the relationship chain, which if found and implemented, can have a dramatic and positive impact on dog/owner relationships. So what is this missing link?

Before I answer, let me ask you a question. In the above examples of undesirable behaviour, what is the common denominator?

In both instances, the dog has decided that either interacting with other dogs or pulling on the lead is more stimulating or more enjoyable than anything that his owner has to offer. This is because the dog has consistently experienced stimulation or enjoyment when partaking in these activities and has never

interactive play guide | 97

been offered an alternative activity that offers a superior level of stimulation or enjoyment. I often hear statements along the lines of: "Max is an angel at home and always does as he is asked". This is an example of the dog/owner relationship superseding any other stimulus present.

For example, when Max is lying on the study floor and his owner calls him, he willingly comes because he desires the affection of his owner more than lying on the floor. He is unlikely to respond in the same way when he is interacting with other dogs. This is because, through experience, Max has learnt that interacting with other dogs is more stimulating than the reward he will receive for returning to his owner. So how can we overcome this?

You guessed it: with interactive play. By creating an interactive play experience and enjoying it on a regular basis, you have the ability to share an activity with your dog that cements your relationship and far outweighs the stimulation and enjoyment value that is offered by playing with other dogs or pulling on the lead.

REMEMBER, IT'S NOT ONLY ABOUT THE TOY

It is important to understand that I am not talking about bribing your dog with his toy whenever he notices another dog or begins to pull on the lead. This would be an easy misunderstanding to make, as the dog's desire for his toy is integral to creating an interactive play experience. However, it is not the only thing that matters, otherwise you will have a dog that is only interested in his toy rather than interacting with his owner.

By following the steps in this book, you are sharing an activity that gives him undeniable proof that you are the creator of maximum stimulation and enjoyment in his life. The toy is an irreplaceable part of the play experience, and its selection is very important.

Your dog will find the toy alone is enjoyable and stimulating, but because of the way you play with him, adjusting your technique to his individual needs, he will find that it becomes so much better when he interacts with you. The toy is a bridge for sharing your interactive play, which will strengthen and add value to you and your dog's relationship. Why is the interactive play experience so powerful?

Let's think about another, more common, reward that we give to our dogs. Food has a high value for dogs, and is used with great success for rewarding all types of behaviours. I use food in training, so I am not criticising its use.

Typically, a dog does something desirable, his behaviour is marked and then he is rewarded with a treat. If this is the case, when does the dog experience the maximum gain from its food reward? Inevitably, this is when he eats the food. So although you supply the food, the dog's maximum pleasure is experienced away from you.

In this example you become a reward supplier, but not the creator, as the pleasure from the reward can be experienced without you.

BECOMING THE CREATOR

Think about your partner surprising you with your favourite type of chocolate. I'm sure we would all be very grateful for the gift and the thought behind it.

As the chocolate is your favourite, you would find it to be delicious and you would enjoy it. If you really wanted that particular type of chocolate and bought yourself it, you would have the same amount of enjoyment as the experience is between you and the chocolate.

Now think about going away on holiday with your partner to a beautiful destination, sharing the most amazing experiences together and both having the time of your life. If you then visited the same holiday destination at a later date and had the same experiences but you were alone, would it be the same? The answer is certain to be in 'no', because you created the first holiday experience with your partner as a team. By creating interactive play that suits you and your dog, you become the creator of an amazingly rewarding activity and experience that you and your dog share as a team, and this cannot be matched.

Remember, the game can only happen when you create it.

By becoming the creator, and not simply the supplier of such a pleasurable and beneficial experience, you will begin to see a marked difference in your dog's general behaviour, such as responsiveness, his willingness to please and his desire to interact with you in general. When you become the creator you will strengthen the great relationship that you already share with your dog.

TWO STEPS TO POSITION YOURSELF AS THE CREATOR

By regularly enjoying interactive play, you will position yourself as the creator in your dog's mind. But there are two simple steps that will help the process even more:

LOVEFORDOGS 80/20 SYSTEM

The Lovefordogs 80/20 system is a practice that can be used on a day-to-day basis and will not only improve your play experience, but also greatly benefits many dog/owner relationships. Before we get on to how it works, let us first consider the walking or exercise pattern of a typical dog. Picture Trixie, who leads the way to the local park as if she were a sled dog with an inbuilt navigation system.

Once Trixie and her owner have arrived at the park, she is let off-lead and proceeds to either run around the park entertaining herself in all sorts of mischievous activities, or finds a group of doggie friends to run around and have fun with. In both scenarios, Trixie is experiencing lots of enjoyment without her owner.

Then when it is time to go home, the owner calls her several times and when Trixie eventually returns, she is clipped on the lead. At this point Trixie's navigational sled dog capability kicks in and she proceeds to lead her owner all the way home.

I have seen examples like this many times and I always ask the question: how big a part did Trixie's owner play in being the source of enjoyment on their walk? Unfortunately, the answer is very little.

Apart from clipping the lead on and off and opening and closing the front door, the owner played very little part in the walk, as all Trixie's enjoyment was experienced without and away from her owner. If this is repeated regularly enough, it will affirm that there are far more enjoyable experiences out there than anything the owner has to offer.

So how does this Lovefordogs 80/20 system work? When exercising your dog, work on the basis that 80 per cent of the exercise time is spent with your dog walking on a loose lead; ideally by your side, but as long as he is not doing a sled dog impression, we are good. The other 20 per cent of your exercise time should be spent partaking in an interactive relationship building activity; your interactive play experience is perfect, but alternatively you can also enjoy some of the interactive exercises suggested in the previous chapter.

Why does this system work? First let's talk about the lead walking; this works so effectively because when your dog walks on a loose lead, his attention is focused on you. Walking in this way, rather than pulling, is a great relationship-sharing activity as the lead walk is about you and your dog – not how quickly he can get to the park.

Once you reach the park or a suitable area, you can then take part in an interactive relationship building activity. This continues to affirm that you are the creator of all the best and most enjoyable experiences, surpassing the surrounding attractions, whatever they may be. This system works so well because it helps to position you as the creator of all the things that your dog likes most in the world.

In your dog's eyes, you are golden.

Interactive play guide | 103

What's the reason for the percentages? As discussed in the previous chapter, your dog's energy levels are hugely relevant to your interactive play sessions, and partaking in interactive activities for too long can work against their development. In contrast, lead walking can be practised for a longer period without any negative side effects. You can, however, divide your 80/20 up in a way that best suits you and your dog, and I would recommend that you do. Make some minor adjustments and see what suits your dog. Working with your dog, and reacting to him will further strengthen your interactive play experience and your overall relationship.

LOVE INDIVIDUAL INTERACTION

If you are reading this book, you must be a dog lover; you may have more than one dog, or you may have friends that have dogs, too. There are also lots of opportunities for meeting dogs and their owners when you take your dog out and about. This is one of the pleasures of owning a dog, and both dogs and humans enjoy the social interaction it brings.

However, it is easy to fall into the natural trend of allowing our dogs to interact with other dogs all of the time. There is no problem at all with dogs interacting with each other, but if your dog is experience a great deal of pleasure from other dogs on a regular basis, what is this affirming in his mind? In most cases, he will be learning that other dogs have more to offer than his owner. When you watch your dog playing with a special doggie friend, where the relationship is relaxed and comfortable, your dog will seem like he's having the time of his life. The problem is that you are not the creator of the experience; in fact you are not even involved it. In this case, your dog's friend is the creator. If this happens too frequently, in your dog's eyes you will lose your creator status. I am certainly not suggesting that your dog doesn't socialise with other dogs. But the interactive time you spend with your dog should outweigh the interactive time he spends with other dogs. Your dog has got to love the individual interaction that you share with him more than anything else; this is a fundamental part of establishing a strong relationship with your dog.

IMPLEMENTING THE TWO STEPS

Individual interaction, on a regular basis, plus working with the 80/20 system, will help you to develop your interactive play experience, and continue to strengthen the relationship that you share with your dog. All it takes is planning. You need to adopt a routine so that both steps become part of your everyday life. When these steps become a habit, you will see the rewards that they offer. These are two very simple adjustments that can greatly benefit you and your dog's relationship; it is often the small but lasting adjustments that will make all the difference.

RELATIONSHIP WRAP UP

A good relationship is a fundamental part of sharing an enjoyable and rewarding life with your dog, regardless of whether he is is a pet companion or your workmate. Your dog needs to see you as the most fun person – the creator of all good things. Interactive play lies at the core of establishing this relationship, and implementing the two-step system will help the process even more.

By putting the information in this chapter in place, you have the ability to strengthen your relationship by becoming the creator of a very unique, enjoyable and stimulating experience that cannot be matched. Remember, always work towards being a creator of the best experience in the world and not simply a reward-supplier.

ACTIVATING THE TOY

When you introduce your dog to the interactive play experience, one of the first steps is to get him interested in engaging, or gripping, the toy you have chosen. You can initially provoke interest in the toy by utilising your dog's natural prey drive or chase instinct – this is the dog's natural desire to chase things that move. I call this the Toy Activation Response or TAR for short.

Activating the toy is a process of animating it (i.e. moving it) so your dog becomes interested in engaging and gripping it. Every dog's TAR level is different; for some minimum effort is required, while for others you will have to work a little harder. What is important is that you develop an understanding of your dog's TAR level so the toy is sufficiently animated that he wants to engage with it. In this chapter I will discuss the different options of how you can go about activating the toy to suit your dog's TAR level. But first, let's talk about avoiding a common mistake that will mar your progress.

STOPPING BEFORE YOU HAVE STARTED

If you are working with a dog that has a high TAR level, activating the toy is seldom an issue as a minimal amount of animation is needed to get him interested and engaged with his toy. On the other hand, if your dog has a lower TAR level, you will have to arouse his interest by making the toy come alive.

How can you make a toy irresistible?

Interactive play guide | 107

It is a case of adjusting and adapting your activation technique to suit your dog or, as I call it, finding your dog's activation buttons. As you practise the activation method that suits your dog, his TAR level will improve. But first we have got to find those activation buttons...

Many people give up almost before they have started because they have convinced themselves that their dog will never be interested in a toy. Think back to our discussions on the importance of belief (see Chapter Four: Energy's Effects).

If you have doubts, you will fail to find your dog's activation buttons, which is all part of the fun of creating an interactive play experience. All it takes is a little persistence, implementing adjustments and adaptations, and sometimes thinking outside the box, to discover which technique suits your dog.

There is nothing to compare with the feeling when you discover the technique for the first time, and your dog becomes captivated by the beginning of interactive play. Not only are you sharing a great sense of achievement, you have also gained a unique understanding of your dog's TAR level along with a full set of toy activation skills that will continue to benefit you and your dog's interactive play experiences.

Some time ago, Mary, and her Cockapoo, Madison, attended one of my workshops. When I asked how I could help, Mary explained that she was struggling to get Madison interested in his toy and she thought there was little chance of creating an interactive play experience. I asked a few questions and suggested that Mary and Madison showed me what they would usually do to begin their play sessions.

As they entered the workspace, I could see that Madison was very interested in all of the wonderful things that the workspace had to offer, despite having visited the area on a regular basis.

Mary activated the toy, and I was really impressed as she did a great job of gaining Madison's attention, particularly when he had shown such interest in his surroundings. So why wouldn't Madison engage with the toy?

Mary activated her toy very close to her body. She succeeded in getting Madison's attention, but he appeared to be confused. He was jumping up at Mary and was very excited, but he was not quite sure whether to seek a cuddle from Mum or engage with the toy. I suggested that she tried an activation extension, which attaches to the toy and allows you to activate and animate the toy away from your body. Mary started working with this, and the change in Madison was quickly apparent.

Why did it work? The simple answer was that when the toy was activated at a distance from Mary's body it cleared up the confusion in his mind as to whether he should engage with the toy or look for cuddles.

Now his focus was on the toy, which he engaged with very quickly, allowing a short period of interaction for invincibility so the session finished on a win. I suggested that Mary practised her new activation technique regularly while beginning to create an interactive play experience. I recommended working in a familiar place, with minimum distractions, which would help Madison's focus and facilitate the development of his TAR.

I also suggested that they started to use a play collar during interactive play sessions (see Chapter Four), which is a game changer. Finally, I explained how to incrementally introduce their interactive play to different environments.

About a month later I received an email with a video attached. The video showed Mary and Madison in a small, grassed area.

Mary was activating her toy, and I could see that Madison's TAR level had at least tripled and as he engaged the toy and began to

A dog's response to a toy revolves around movement.

Interactive play guide | 111

play. It was the smile on Mary's face and the visible enjoyment that Madison was experiencing that made me so happy – interactive play had worked its magic again. So remember, don't stop before you have started: adjust, adapt and conquer!

THE ART OF ACTIVATION

The real question, here, is how do you activate your toy in a way that suits your dog? Mastering the art of activation is the answer: let me explain how. The aim of the game is to ignite your dog's TAR, which means you have got to make the toy irresistible. Remembering that your dog's TAR level revolves around movement, you need to ignite and utilise his natural chase response.

What type of movement? Think about times when you watched two sociable dogs – those happy-go-lucky types – chasing each other around and playing. If you observe closely you will see a number of commonalities.

Often, before the chase begins, the dog that is going to be chased ('the chased') will use just enough movement to tease and ignite 'the chaser's' interest.

This often takes several attempts with what, can best be described as 'catch me if you can', close-up, teasing movements, which consist of 'the chased' moving in and out of 'the chaser's' range of contact, without being caught.

Once 'the chased' has ignited enough interest for the chase to begin, he will set off running, maintaining enough speed and movement so that 'the chaser' knows he can catch up, but he still has to work to reach his playmate.

This will generally be the case, regardless of the difference in the two dogs' speed capability. The chase is rarely in a straight line; more often 'the chased' will make unexpected, unconventional movements with sudden directional changes, running in circles and S shapes, zig-zagging and executing quick turns.

Then, before 'the chaser' loses interest, 'the chased' slows down just enough so that he can be caught and close-up interaction can begin.

The dog's motivation to get the toy is key but he must think that it is achievable.

Our dogs offer us the best information and knowledge available, and we can make good use of this when activating a toy. When you start, the toy needs to be activated with enough speed and movement so as it draws your dog's interest and teases him into engaging. 'Enough' is the most important word here, because if you don't bring enough speed and movement into play, you will fail to gain your dog's interest.

On other hand, if you use too much speed and movement, particularly in the developmental stages of your interactive play experience, your dog may feel that engaging the toy is too difficult a task and not worth his while to attempt. The art is to activate the toy with enough speed and movement so that your dog feels he has to work to engage or catch the toy, but he does not see it as an unachievable task.

When activating the toy, use unconventional movements; move the toy in and out of his contact range in different directions and formations, teasing him with the toy and making it super interesting. Think back to the canine cha cha, described in Chapter One.

Your toy activation needs to involve the same rhythm and energy as we use for the dance; it has got to be fun and interesting for you and your dog. Also bear in mind the impact of your body language and the need for positive energy, as they will both help when it comes to mastering the art of activation.

Once you have ignited your dog's interest in the toy, keep it moving but slow the pace so he can engage or catch the toy. From your dog's perspective, the game is more fun if he catches the toy on the move rather than being given it. This will also help when it comes to maintaining engagement with the toy for his interaction for invincibility.

If you freeze the toy the moment your dog shows interest, it may well kill his enthusiasm for the game. He has to perceive catching the toy during activation as super interesting, a little challenging but very achievable and, most of all, it has got to be fun for both of you.

If you can get your dog to engage with the toy through movement, you are on your way to establishing interactive play. But what if your dog shows little or no interest in the toy, even when you are moving it?

ACTIVATION ACCELERATORS

As we know, every dog's TAR level is different, meaning that every handler's activation technique will be different depending on the adjustments and adaptations made to suit their dog.

If your dog has a naturally low TAR level, you will need to use different methods of activating the toy, which will accelerate your results – I call these activation accelerators. These techniques will help you customise your activation process to suit your dog, giving you every chance of success. Let's look at the options:

ARM'S LENGTH ACTIVATION

This is one the most popular methods of toy activation, if not the most popular. All you need to do is hold the toy and activate it at arm's length to gain your dog's interest and begin the interactive play experience. This is the chosen method of toy activation for most handlers as it allows maximum flexibility; you can carry the toy in a pocket and instigate a game where, and when, it suits you and your dog.

The majority of dogs take to this type of activation very well and experience no issues with it. But if your dog is struggling with this method, you can make some adjustments to your technique, which should have a positive impact. What are they?

The clue is in the title. If you make a conscious effort to activate your toy at arm's length, away from your body, with loose arms, it will give you a diversity of rhythm and freedom of movement which will enhance the toy's value.

It may help if you envisage an orchestra conductor, using a baton. His movements are choreographed to direct the orchestra, but they are flowing and natural as he interprets the music.

This method of toy activation may not succeed if the toy is too close to the handler's body. This can restrict the handler's

Activating the toy at arm's length works well for most dogs.

ability to activate the toy with the diversity, rhythm and freedom of movement that is needed to gain their dog's attention.

As I mentioned earlier, the dog can also become confused in this situation, mistaking close-up toy activation with an invitation for a cuddle. Arm's length activation is the end goal of most handlers. However, if you cannot ignite your dog's interest with this method, there is no need to worry – I have some more activation accelerators that can help.

ACTIVATION EXTENSIONS

The purpose of an activation extension is to allow you to activate the toy away from your body so you can use more diversity, rhythm and freedom of movement than would be possible if you were holding and activating it at arm's length. The beauty of an activation extension is that you remain fully in control of the toy's movement, but you can be more creative. Think of yourself as a fly fisherman casting for salmon in an icy river.

I started using this technique by attaching a toy to a long lunge whip – the type used for schooling horses. This served me well for many years, but I have now swapped it for a flirt pole. In effect, this is a modified version of a lunge whip that has been designed and manufactured specifically as an activation extension.

A flirt pole consists of a lightweight pole with a handle at one end and a length of elasticated cord attached to the other, where you attach the toy. It serves the same purpose as the lunge whip but is much lighter and the handle is shorter, which makes it more comfortable and easier to use for the art of activation.

Another activation extension technique is to attach a light line to your toy. Alternatively, you can make use of a readymade version which consists of a toy with a light line attached. This gives the opportunity to experiment with toys of different shapes and sizes (see Chapter Three: Toy selection). This type of activation extension is really useful as it serves the same purpose as a flirt pole but you can fold it away in a jacket pocket. However, some handlers find a flirt pole gives more control. When using a light line, some dogs have a tendency to engage with the line rather than the toy.

The activation extension you choose comes down to personal preference and, again, it is a case of adjusting and adapting your methods and techniques to suit you and your dog. To

An activation extension allows you to be more creative.

stack the odds in your favour, I suggest that you master your activation process and develop your dog's TAR level with the flirt pole. Once your dog's TAR level is increasing, and he fires into action when you activate the toy, you can switch to a light line extension.

By this stage you will have honed your fly-fly fishing art of activation technique so using the light line will come more naturally. Your dog will have been consistently engaging his toy during your interactive play sessions and will be far less likely to engage the light line when you switch over.

The light line often serves as the bridge between using an activation extension and transferring to a standard toy as you can incrementally decrease the extent of the light line as your dog's TAR level develops. In time, you will be able to detach the toy and introduce arm's length activation. However, this is not a prerequisite. Many handlers choose to stick with an activation extension as this suits their interactive play experience. Remember it is always a case of adjusting and adapting to suit you and your dog.

TIPS FOR USING AN ACTIVATION EXTENSION

If you are experimenting with an activation extension, you need to consider how to operate it in order to spark your dog's interest.

At the beginning of your activation process, use the full length of the extension and activate the toy very close to the ground. It may seem more natural to dangle the toy or activate it in mid air, but this hinders the accuracy of what you are doing. I have also noticed that a dog with low TAR levels is more likely to be stimulated when the toy is at ground level, and will give quicker more determined response than when the toy is activated in mid air.

Now you are ready to engage with your dog. The controlled use of an activation extension is all in the flick of the wrist. You will use more than your wrist when activating the toy, but if you keep the flick of your wrist in mind, it produces movement that most dogs find irresistible.

I have used these methods on many occasions with great success, particularly when helping dogs that have very low TAR levels. The technique may take a little practice to master but it is all part of the fun and you and your dog will love the journey.

THROW FOR ACTIVATION

Dogs that have a low TAR level will often respond when a toy, commonly a ball, is thrown for them in a game of fetch. I have seen dogs suddenly spring to life and race to fetch a ball when they previously showed no desire to engage the toy at all. This is because the sudden speed of movement ignites the dog's TAR and then the ball naturally slows down to be engaged.

This is the same series of movements that I described earlier, but throwing a ball prolongs the experience. The problem can be that when your dog engages the toy, he let's go or loses interest as soon as the toy stops moving. If this is the case, don't see it as a problem – quite the reverse. You should view it as a blessing as you have created an activation foundation to build on.

The question is how do you change the game of chasing a ball across a field – and not bringing it back – into a successful activation technique which is part of your interactive play experience?

The first thing you need to think about is distance. Generally

Throwing the toy can stimulate a dog with low arousal.

you would throw the ball or toy a considerable way, but this can be counter productive. If the toy is thrown too far, you cannot develop your dog's TAR level because you are too far away to help.

Your dog will also run out of energy if has to repeatedly chase after his toy over a distance, and may lose interest in it (see Chapter Four: Energy's effects). You will also tire if you have to keep running back and forth to collect the toy if the dog doesn't engage and retrieve it.

So my first suggestion is to decrease the distance when you throw the toy. Bear in mind, it is the speed of the toy leaving your hand that ignites your dog's TAR, and if you throw the ball with force, it will naturally go a long way. So how do you resolve this? Our natural throwing technique is up and away, rather like a javelin thrower, where the aim is to create distance.

But if you change your technique, so you throw as if you were skimming a stone, it will make a big difference. The toy will leave your hand at speed but it will slow down at a quicker rate as it makes contact with the ground which will, in turn, decrease the distance it travels. Throwing distance should be customised to suit your individual dog but, generally speaking, a distance of 15 metres is sufficient.

The quick release combined with the skimming action is stimulating for your dog as the toy remains active for a short period while at ground level rather than coming to a complete stop as it lands, which happens when you throw javelin-style. Think of a merry-go-round; it is much more fun when it is spinning. In this context, you, as handler, just need to make sure that you are the one that is spinning the wheel. Before you start work on perfecting your throwing technique, you will need to do a little DIY adaptation on your toy to ensure success.

All you will need is a length of strong, thin climbing cord that is approximately 2 metres longer than your throwing distance. So, if a 15-metre distance suits your dog, you will need a cord that is 17 metres in length. Now attach your interactive toy to the cord, as safely and securely as possible. Take particular care not to tie the cord around the body of the toy where the dog will engage.

I often use this technique with a ball on a rope as it is easy to tie the cord to rope handle. But as we discussed earlier (Chapter Three: Toy Selection), it is essential that your interactive toy, no matter what you choose, has a handle or a place where you can hold it, which will be where you attach the cord. Now you are ready to begin:

- Hold the end of the cord with your non-throwing hand, and hold the toy in your other hand.

- Activate your dog's TAR by throwing the toy, but using the new throwing technique, discussed above.

- As the toy comes to a natural stop, use the cord to draw the toy back towards you. As you do this, use a flicking motion generated from your wrist. Work at keeping the movements of the toy active and exciting in order to maintain your dog's interest, even though you are working at a distance. This will encourage him to engage with the toy because it now remains activated while at a distance, whereas previously it came to a stop on landing.

- Once your dog has engaged or gripped the toy, work on your interaction for invincibility. It doesn't matter if your dog is at a distance of 10 metres at this stage. Begin your even tug of war at this distance and incrementally work your way closer to your dog, at a pace and over a period of time that suits him. Try hard not to rush.

- As this process develops, your dog will begin to engage the toy very soon after it makes contact with the ground. He will also learn that he has more fun when he engages the toy and experiences interactive play. As this becomes apparent, use the art of activation to stimulate your dog and activate his TAR before you throw the toy, while incrementally shortening the distance that you throw it.

- As you progress, you will notice that your dog begins to engage the toy very soon after you have activated it and thrown it. When this happens, you can reduce the length of the cord and follow the guidelines for activation extensions.

If you follow these steps, you will have utilised your dog's natural abilities and moulded them in to an activation process, creating your interactive play experience.

ACTIVATION LOCATION

If your dog has a naturally low TAR level when you first begin your toy activation process, you may find that activation location – where you instigate interactive play – is influential.

Let me explain. If you have been experiencing some challenges in igniting your dog's interest in the toy, I would suggest starting your activation process in a controlled and familiar environment, with very little distraction (for example, the back garden). You want your dog to feel comfortable in the environment, with the minimum of distraction so he will focus on you.

This should always be viewed as a top priority as once your dog begins to focus, success will follow. Stacking the odds in your favour will give you a far better chance of gaining his attention than if he is either worried or stimulated by his surroundings. In all situations, your aim is to make the task easy and achievable. A neutral environment will also help you as a handler, giving you the time and opportunity to hone your skills and adjust and adapt your technique in a way that will suit your dog and develop his TAR level.

In time, you will reach a point where you will consistently gain your dog's attention when you activate the toy.

Consistency is key here; you need to have consistency in your dog's toy activation response so that every time you activate the toy, you are confident that your dog will respond and engage with it.

You need to have that consistent response before moving on to the next step because if your dog is only sporadically engaging the toy in a familiar environment, it lessens the chance of success in a new environment.

The time that it takes to get a consistent response will be different for every dog, but remember to love the process and enjoy the experience. When you have built up consistency, lasting results are far more likely. In this situation, you will find that using a play collar to condition your dog is highly beneficial.

OK, so your dog is now consistently responding to your toy activation process and his TAR level is developing. What's next? You can now begin to incrementally introduce your activation process to different environments. For example, start by going to a place that your dog has visited many times before, such as your local park or the training hall that you may visit once a week.

Rather than going to a busy space in the park or getting to the hall as class is beginning, opt to find a quieter spot in the park or get to your class a half hour early. In this way you are introducing new environments but managing the amount of distraction, which sets you and your dog up for success.

Working in a familiar environment is helpful for some dogs.

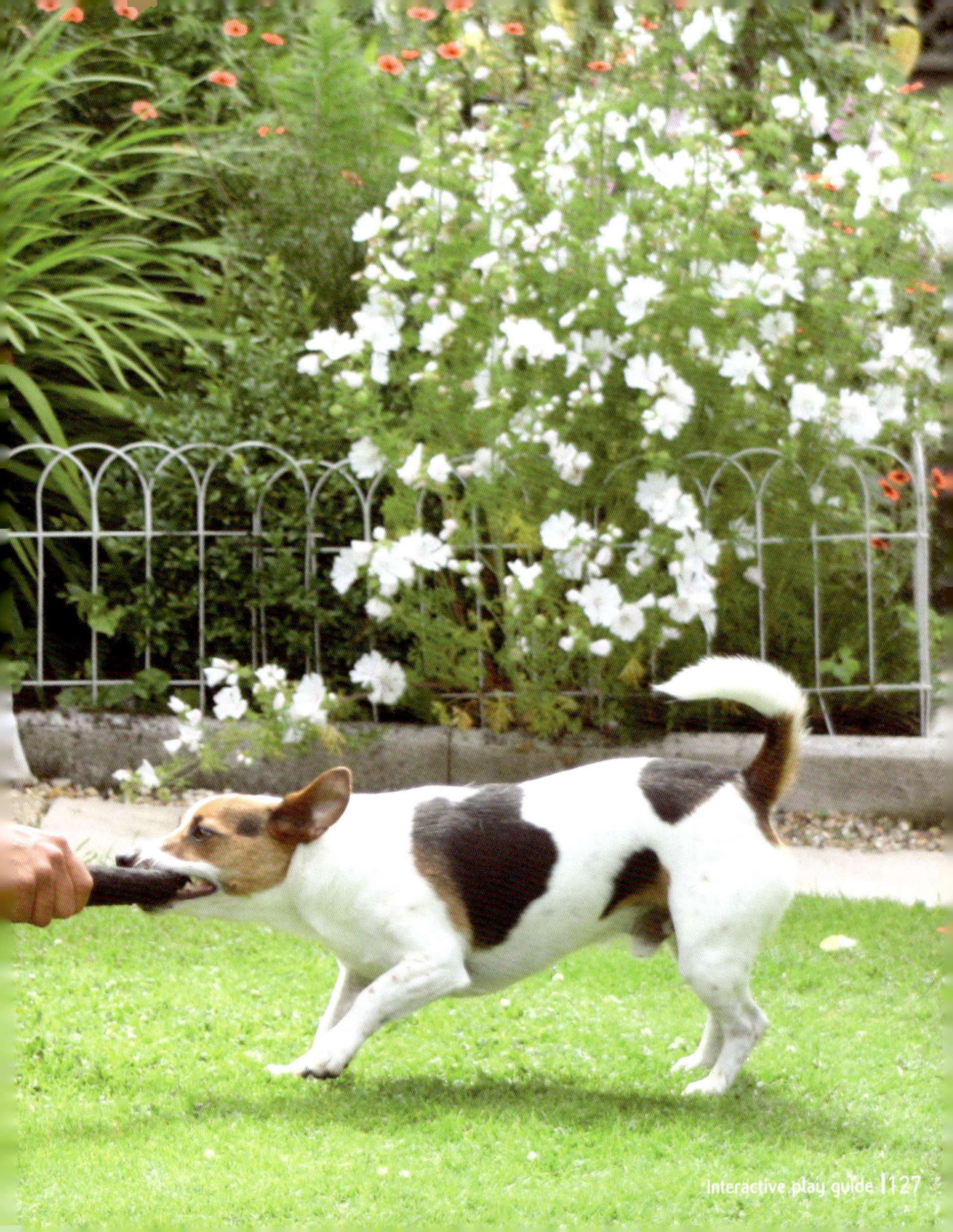

The location may have changed, but you still need to follow exactly the same activation process as you conducted in your familiar environment.

It is important to clear your mind and activate your toy as before, without allowing doubts and negative energy to creep in. You need to concentrate on having fun with your dog. As your dog responds to your toy activation, do not be tempted to push the session too far.

Instead, capitalise on the success by allowing your dog to win the toy so he has the chance to interact for invincibility. Follow the same procedure whenever you introduce a new environment; set yourself up for success and always finish on a win.

As this process develops, you will be able to incrementally increase your interaction time, always working at your dog's pace. As your dog continues to develop, introduce distractions to the different environments. If your dog is super friendly, and previously had no interest in the toy when people were around, introduce people, one or two at a time, initially keeping some distance from your activation area.

Then slowly, over a period of time, close the distance and incrementally increase the numbers at a pace that suits your dog. By covering the steps in this section you will be able to work towards introducing your activation process and your interactive play experience to all of the environments that you desire.

Remember, always consciously think to move in incremental steps that suit your dog and end every session with success, on a win. Keeping this in mind will make activation in any location possible.

LAST THOUGHTS ON ACTIVATING THE TOY

In this chapter we have talked about what you need to do to develop your dog's TAR level and how to establish a solid toy activation process, using activation accelerators to overcome problems that can arise in the activation process.

The advice and information given here should be read in conjunction with Chapter Two: Non-Verbal Communication and Chapter Four: Energy's Effects as the material covered in these chapters is key to the activation process and the development of a dog's TAR level. When I am running workshops, I find that toy activation is often overlooked by handlers. However, I see it as the cornerstone of the interactive play experience and would urge every handler to give it due consideration.

CONTROL DURING INTERACTIVE PLAY

What do I mean by control? My favourite description of the word is: 'the ability to influence or direct behaviour or the course of events'.

The reason I like this description is because it relates specifically to the use of control during interactive play. When control is discussed in relation to dogs, it can become both complex and controversial. But rather than getting bogged down with theories that are difficult to understand and even harder to implement, I want to break down our control conversation into a few simple subjects that are designed to fit into your interactive play experience.

TEACHING YOUR DOG TO LOVE TO LET GO

I have started with this subject because teaching the 'let go' or 'leave' is a common cause of problems for both dog and handler. The goal is to teach your dog to willingly let go of his toy when you ask.

This is important because it avoids the conflict that can be associated with the request to "leave" and the toy possession issues that may result, which will both have a negative effect on interactive play experiences.

Ending the game should not be a negative experience.

If your dog is happy to let go of his toy on request, you can focus on having fun, without tension or stress on either side. How do you achieve this?

For many dogs, letting go of the toy signals the end of a pleasurable experience. This is not an unwarranted perception on the dog's part, as through repetition, he has learnt that when he lets go of his toy, the fun stops.

To add insult to injury, nothing is offered in return for the co-operation he has shown in letting go of his favourite toy. If this cycle is repeated too many times, the dog will decide that the better option is to hang on to his toy and so start the problem of toy possession, which is not conducive to creating an amazing interactive play experience.

We can't really blame our dogs for not wanting the fun to stop; it's a normal reaction. Think back to the best holiday you have ever had – can you picture it?

You are probably remembering a particular experience on that holiday when you were having the most fun – maybe going on a special trip or doing something really exciting that you had never done before.

Now imagine that at the point when you where having the most fun, you were told you had to return home right away? How would you feel?

The chances are that you might return home depending on the circumstances, but there is a good chance that you would not be overjoyed about it. That is, unless the thought of returning to your family, your canine companions and all the comforts of home, were to ignite the same feeling of enjoyment that you where experiencing while on holiday.

The secret is to teach your dog to *love* to let go of his toy when you ask, so it is always the best option to choose. You can do this this by making the 'let go' part of the pleasurable experience that you have created.

Refer back to Chapter Five when you became the 'creator' of the interactive play experience. In just the same way, the 'let go' will become part of your interactive play experience and something that both you and your dog will enjoy.

Let's get started on the steps to teach your dog to love to let go.

USING A PINPOINT WORD

When teaching the 'let go' I have found that using a pinpoint word is massively beneficial. A pinpoint word works on the same principle as a clicker; it gives you the ability to mark and reward the exact moment when your dog lets go of his toy, which makes the exercise much easier for your dog to understand.

If you have been using clicker training previously and your dog already understands the concept, you can implement your existing skills into teaching the love to let go. However, you may need to adjust and adapt to whatever suits you and your dog best.

For those new to clicker training, I will give a brief explanation, keeping scientific terms to a minimum, as I am all about actionable, easy-to-understand steps to success. OK here goes: we are going to pair a primary reinforcer, or reward, with our pinpoint word, which will lead to the pinpoint word becoming a conditioned reinforcer or reward. If you don't quite understand yet it's no problem, it will all become clear as we talk through the steps:

- Choose a pinpoint word; something short and simple works really well, words such as win, yes and OK are popular.

How can you control play without killing enthusiasm?

interactive play guide | 135

- Now pair the pinpoint word with a primary reinforcer, such as a high value food reward, cut into small treat-size portions. I often find this pairing is best done in a familiar area with the minimum of distractions – somewhere like the kitchen.

- Start by holding a piece of the high value food reward in one hand so it is clearly visible to the dog. In all probability he will reach for the treat so, as he does so, say your pinpoint word and then give him the reward.

- After repeating this over a few short sessions, the dog learns that the pinpoint word is followed by the reward. When this happens your pinpoint word has become a conditioned reinforcer or reward.

It's best to work on this pairing before teaching your dog to love to let go, as the use of a conditioned reinforcer will prove massively beneficial for you and your dog during the learning process.

PICK YOUR 'LET GO' WORD

This process requires few words, but the choice of word is important. It may sound really simple – and it is – but let me explain the significance. If you pick one single word, and use it consistently when teaching your dog to let go, it will make the process easier for you and your dog. All too often a handler starts by asking the dog for "out" and if the dog doesn't let go, they follow up by using the dog's name: "Jack, out".

If that doesn't work, the handler puts in a different command altogether: "Jack, I said leave", and the dog might let go. I know I would be a little confused at this stage, which means there is a pretty good chance that the dog is equally baffled. The question is: which word did Jack associate with letting go? As handlers we, unconsciously, string words together; they mean something to us – but are meaningless as far as the dog is concerned. The simplicity of consciously choosing one word, and consistently using it when asking your dog to let go, will benefit you and your dog. A little tip: I have often found that one-syllable words work very well for both owner and dog.

A FAIR TRADE

When you are teaching your dog to love to let go of the toy, you need to offer a fair trade reward. What I mean by this is that you must offer him a fair trade for the toy that it he is holding in his mouth with something that equals the toy's value to induce him to let go.

There are two common trades that have a consistent history of success: the first is a toy that is identical to the one that your dog is holding in his mouth; the second is an extremely high value food reward.

This needs to be whatever is your dog's absolute favourite food in the world – ideally something he only receives as a real treat from time to time. The secret of success is in how the trade is offered.

USING A MATCHING TOY AS YOUR FAIR TRADE

Let's start with how to offer your dog a matching toy as an inducement to let go of the toy in his mouth. Your dog has engaged your toy and you are interacting together; you also have a matching toy ready for a fair trade swap. This needs to be easy to access and on your person, for example in a big pocket.

During your interaction you will let go of the toy, allowing your dog to win the even tug of war and leaving him with the toy in his mouth. As soon as you have let go, immediately animate your body, via non-verbal communication, whilst moving

The toy you offer must be of equal value – or even better – than the toy you have been using for your interactive game.

138 | Interactive play guide

backwards and away from your dog. As you are doing this, produce and present your fair trade toy. To do this effectively, you will need to use your activation skills and your non-verbal communication to make the fair trade toy and the experience that you offering more desirable than the toy that your dog is holding.

Remember, you are the creator of the experience and the interactive play toy is part of the experience. This will generally result in your dog running towards you and letting go of the toy because of his desire to engage the fair trade toy which you are now activating.

In fact, in your dog's eyes you are offering more than a fair trade as the 'new' toy involves an interactive play experience which has far more attraction than a toy that has become boring without your interaction.

As soon as your dog lets go of the toy that he was holding in his mouth, say your pinpoint word to reinforce the action of letting go. This needs to be as accurate as possible, ideally saying the pinpoint word at exactly the same time as the dog opens his mouth and lets go of the toy. Make sure your dog is able to engage the fair trade toy that you are activating very quickly after using your pinpoint word, and once he has it, be sure to spend a short period of time taking part in some quality interaction with him. If you have worked through the steps outlined above, your dog will recognise the pinpoint word as a conditioned reinforcer or reward.

For the purpose of teaching the let go, we have simply replaced the high value food reward that we used to condition the pinpoint word with the reward of engaging with the fair trade toy and interacting with you.

You are effectively pinpointing and rewarding your dog's

decision to open his mouth and let go of the toy he was holding. This method has a proven track record as the dog is not being short-changed – he is learning to love the let go. Your dog has now released the toy he was holding, which you have pinpointed and rewarded.

He is now engaged with the second toy and you are interacting with him. What next? You should aim to interact in an even tug of war for around 10 seconds, trying to stay in roughly the same location where your fair trade took place.

Let your dog win the toy, and move as quickly as possible to the toy that your dog has recently abandoned. Pick up the static toy and repeat the process, with another energy filled activation.

Finish on a keen let go, at a point where your dog is still engaged in the let go game. The number of times you repeat this is really dependent on Mount Energy, which we discussed in Chapter Four.

Certainly for the first session, a successful let go that is repeated once or twice is plenty. It is better to repeat the love to let go process little and often, incrementally increasing the number per session over a period of time that suits your dog. This is important because if you attempt the let go too many times in a session, particularly in the early stages, you run the risk of your dog becoming fatigued and not wanting to let go.

ALWAYS FINISH ON A WIN

Before we move on to the next step of teaching your dog to love to let go, I want to stress the importance of ending all of your play sessions on a win, win basis. As you are developing the love to let go, it is crucial that on the last let go of every session your dog receives a fair trade reward. This may seem obvious, but is something we have to consciously take on board.

Why is that? If you analyse the interaction, you are rewarding your dog's let go action with engagement and interaction of a fair trade toy. When you finish the fair trade game your dog will naturally have one of the two toys in his mouth.

To finish the game, you need to put both toys away. So how do you reward that last let go and finish the game with your dog having a toy in his mouth? A natural reaction would be to finish your game by putting the fair trade toy away as your dog does his last let go of the session.

However, this would mean that your dog receives nothing for his final let go effort. This can go against all the good work you have done in your session as you are not finishing on a win. So, the way to get round this is to swap the last let go for an extremely high value fair trade food reward. In this way, you finish the game with both toys in your possession and your dog ends the session being rewarded with his favorite treat. It's a win, win way to end the game.

PAIRING THE LET GO WORD WITH THE LET GO

Your dog will soon begin to understand the game and love to let go of the toy he is holding in return for the reward of interacting with you. When the let go becomes consistent, you will be ready to pair the let go word with the dog's action of letting go.

Up until this point, you have used the activation of the fair trade toy as a cue to induce your dog to let go of the toy he is holding, and have then pinpointed and rewarded the action. You are now going to fade out the degree of toy activation that has been the cue for letting go, and substitute the let go word. How are we going to do it? It's not hard if you follow these simple steps:

- After repeating the first part of the love to let go process over a few sessions your dog will understand the concept and really to love to let go – so much so, that you get to know the point at which your dog lets go of the toy he is holding. For example, you notice that your dog has began consistently letting go of the toy when you produce your fair trade toy from your pocket.

- Now say the let go word just before your dog lets go – and then continue as before, pinpointing and rewarding the action. So, if your dog lets go of the toy as you produce the fair trade toy from your pocket, say your let go word, (I will use "loose" for the purpose of explaining the process), just before you present the toy. Then, as your dog lets go of the toy, you can pinpoint and reward your dog's action of letting go in exactly the same way as you did previously.

- As the let go word starts to become the cue for your dog to let go of his toy, you can begin to incrementally fade out the visual cues of producing and activating the fair trade toy. For example, if your dog is consistently letting go of his toy once the fair trade toy has been produced and you say "loose", you now need to hold the fair trade toy closer and closer to your body when you say the let go word. Remember to be super consistent with using your pinpoint word to reinforce your dog's action of letting go, and then reward immediately afterwards by presenting the fair trade toy for an interactive game. If you work at this, you will not need to produce or activate the fair trade toy – your dog will respond to the let go word alone.

- At this point your let go word will be the only cue you need for your dog to let go. But it is important to remember that you must always use your pinpoint word and reward on every let go to reinforce the message. This paints a clear picture in the dog's mind and helps to maintain the love to let go.

FOOD FOR YOUR FAIR TRADE

Using food as fair trade can be equally effective in teaching your dog to love to let go. Let's talk through the steps to success. The first point is the type of food to use.

The food needs to be of extremely high value to your dog – and I am sure that most if not every dog owner has a pretty good idea of what floats their dog's boat. Whatever this is, providing it does not have a negative effect on your dog's health, use it. Now you have your high value food rewards, cut them into pieces around the thickness of a pound coin, and roughly the same size and shape as your dog's nose. No need to spend hours crafting perfect shapes but aim to work to these guidelines.

Before you head off to get your dog, put the treats in a pocket that is easy for you to access, but out of your dog's vision. A purpose-made training jacket, or a jacket with big pockets, works well, as you need to avoid fumbling when you are extracting the treats. It will also prove really beneficial if your dog wears his conditioning collar or a very soft and comfortable collar with a light line connected. This prevents your dog trotting away and engaging in that game of cat and mouse that we can never win (see Chapter One: Interaction for Invincibility).

Now to get started:

- Once your dog has engaged the toy, get involved in a short interactive game (shorter than usual) of about 10 seconds' duration.

- When the time is up, let your dog win the toy and allow him to parade his toy in a small circle while you hold the light line. Now encourage your dog to come to you, holding the toy in his mouth. It would be a good idea to refresh your memory by looking back over Chapter One: Interaction for Invincibility.

For many dogs, a high-value treat is regarded as a very reasonable swap for a toy.

- So now your dog is back with you and holding the toy proudly in his mouth. Let him settle in a position alongside you where he feels most comfortable. It is really important that your dog feels relaxed and that there is no conflict between you and your dog, as this will compromise the following love to let go steps.

- Once your dog is settled in a position of his choosing, you are going to share some affection. I do this by smoothing an area of the dog's body with the flat of my hand. You need to be slow and rhythmical and smooth an area of the body that your dog finds desirable so that he is calm and enjoys the interaction.

- Now take a piece of food from your pocket with the hand that is not smoothing your dog. Gently place the treat over your dog's nose, so that the food is making contact with his nostrils. The positioning of the food is very important. The gentle touch of the food on the dog's nose, coupled with influx of appetising scent, will cause the dog to open his mouth, almost by reflex, to eat the treat. If you dangle the food near your dog's nose or in front of it, you are unlikely to get the same reaction.

- As soon as your dog opens his mouth, letting go of the toy to eat the treat, say your pinpoint word to reinforce the action of letting go. You need to be as accurate as possible with this pairing, ideally saying your pinpoint word at exactly the same time as your dog opens his mouth and lets go of the toy. Immediately after saying your pinpoint word, give your dog the high value food reward. This accurately pinpoints and rewards your dog's action of letting go of his toy, using the same principle as when using a fair trade toy.

- You can then activate your toy and repeat the process. The number of times you do this is dependent on your dog and Mount Energy. Certainly for the first session, a successful let go repeated a couple of times is plenty. It is better to repeat this love to let go process little and often, incrementally increasing the number in a session over a period of time that suits your dog. Remember, always stack all of the odds in your favour and finish on a win.

PAIRING THE WORD WITH ACTION WHEN USING FAIR TRADE FOOD

Your dog will soon begin to understand this fair trade swap and love to let go of the toy he is holding in return for a delicious treat. When the let go becomes consistent, you are ready to pair your let go word with the dog's action of letting go.

Up to this point, you have used the action of placing the high value food reward on your dog's nose as a cue to open his mouth and eat the food, which also results in letting go of the toy. You have then been pinpointing and rewarding the action.

You are now going to fade out the presentation of food as a visual and sensory cue for letting go and add your let go word as the cue instead.

- After repeating the first part of the love to let go process over a few sessions, your dog will probably let go of his toy before you place the food reward on his nose. Note the exact point he lets go: for example, he may consistently let go of his toy when the food reward is approximately 10cm from his nose.

- Aim to say the let go word just before your dog lets go of his toy and then, as before, pinpointing and rewarding the action. For example, if your dog lets go of the toy when the food reward is 10cm from his nose, produce the treat and say "loose" just before the food reaches this point. Then as your dog lets go of the toy, pinpoint and reward the action of letting go in exactly the same way as before.

- ` As your let go word begins to become the cue for your dog to let go of his toy, you need to incrementally fade out the presentation of the food reward as a cue for letting go and replace it with your let go word. For example, if your dog is consistently letting go of the toy as you say "loose" when the food is approximately 10cm from his nose, you need to work on increasing the distance so that the treat is further from your dog's nose when you say your let go word. Be consistent with using your pinpoint word to reinforce your dog's action of letting go and then rewarding immediately afterwards. In this way, you will no longer need to produce the food as the let go word has become the cue instead.

- Remember to use your pinpoint word and reward on every let go to reinforce and reward the dog's action of letting go.

VEERING FROM THE FAIR TRADE PATH

We have now covered all the steps needed to get your dog to love to let go when you ask. As previously discussed, you may need to make minor adjustments and adaptations to customise either system to suit your dog's needs, but the steps and the fair trade concept are the key to loving to let go success.

Once your dog is loving to let go of his toy when you ask, it is very easy to unconsciously start veering from the fair trade path.

Let me explain. I have helped more people than I can remember with the love to let go process and it is great to receive messages of how well their dog has picked up the concept. However, the concept can become a victim of its own success if it works so reliably that we stop offering a fair trade after every let go. This is most likely to occur at the end of an interactive play sessions when the dog lets go of the toy for the last time, and the handler puts the toy away without pinpointing and rewarding his effort. If this happens consistently, it is not long before the dog begins to doubt a fair trade is on offer and no longer buys into the process. Lack of consistency is a handler's biggest challenge. If you stay consistent, stick to the system and always keep the fair trade concept in mind, you will stack all the odds in your favour so you and your dog can achieve love to let go success.

STARTING AND FINISHING YOUR INTERACTIVE PLAY SESSIONS

Interactive play is an activity that requires focus and energy on the part of both you and your dog. You both need to be fully engaged throughout the play sessions. By teaching your dog simple cues for the start and finish of the game, you can avoid a lot of confusion and wasted energy that can tarnish the interactive experience.

STARTING THE GAME

The cue to start the game can be as simple and easy to apply as you like, and I would suggest that a simple start cue will work best. We have already talked about using an interactive play collar to focus your dog's energy on the interactive play experience, and it would be a good idea to go back over that section to refresh your memory.

The conditioning collar is a really easy way to start (and finish) your interactive play sessions, enabling maximum focus and engagement during the session and avoiding wasted energy. The secret is that the interactive play collar concept is simple; your dog will begin to associate your personalised cue with the beginning of your interactive play experience. If you are consistent with using this cue your dog will come to understand the game doesn't start until the cue is implemented, which

A conditioning collar indicates the start of an interactive play session.

Play is quickly underway.

Interactive play guide | 149

allows you to effectively control the start of your interactive play sessions without time wasting or confusion. I understand that not everyone wants to use a collar and there are other options. Many of my clients use a play harness, and some use an interactive play word to pinpoint the beginning of their play sessions, and these work in exactly the same way as a conditioning collar. If you decide on using a word for the start of your interactive play sessions, make sure you choose something unfamiliar or uncommon that you are not likely to say at any other time in your dog's company. If you use the word at other times, your dog will be highly confused when a play session does not ensue and, equally, it becomes ineffective as a cue when you want to start an interactive game. Some of my favorite choices for start words are old cartoon characters or a word from a different language.

FINISHING THE GAME

Once you have decided on the cue that you are going to use to start your interactive play sessions, you need to pick a cue to finish the game. If you have decided to go with an interactive play collar as your cue to begin your game, you also have the means of ending the session on cue.

When it is time to finish, and you have implemented your final fair trade swap for the toy that your dog is holding, you can simply place the toy out of sight and then remove your dog's interactive play collar. If you consistently follow this routine, your dog will soon form the association that once the collar is removed the game is finished. The concept remains the same: no interactive play collar, no interactive play. It is a simple and effective, all-in-one method that can be used to focus your dog on his interactive play sessions while giving you the ability to control the beginning and end of each session. I am a big advocate of the collar, but there are always other options.

How do you end a game when your dog is highly aroused?

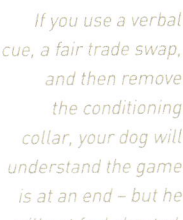

If you use a verbal cue, a fair trade swap, and then remove the conditioning collar, your dog will understand the game is at an end – but he will not feel cheated.

Interactive play guide | 151

It is all about adjusting and adapting the system to suit you and your dog. If you decide to use another piece of equipment, such as a harness, as your personalised cue, the concept will work in exactly the same way. You will need to remove the harness consistently at the finish of your sessions so your dog realises that this is the signal that tells him play is at an end. If you have decided to use a word as the cue to finish your interactive play sessions, again, you need to choose something that is not part of your everyday vocabulary. My personal favourite to end the game is "finito", the beautiful Italian version of the word. The concept remains exactly the same as when using a collar, with some minor adjustments. For example, when it is time to finish your interactive play session, and you have made the final fair trade swap for the toy that your dog is holding, place the toy out of sight and reach, and say your finish word. Just as your dog learns to associate the start word with the beginning of your interactive play session, so he will learn that the finish word ends the session. The finish word must be applied consistently so the dog understands that once he hears the finish word, there will be no more play.

THE WRAP UP ON CONTROL

In this chapter we have talked about how to overcome the confusion that can surround control. We have seen that control is relevant and can be used as part of your interactive play experience to benefit you and your dog. Remember, the best description for the word control is: the ability to influence or direct behaviour or the course of events. That is what we are aiming for. As a partner in interactive play sessions, your goals are to teach your dog to love to let go, and to start and end a play session without conflict or confusion.

On that note, I can think of no better way to end the chapter than to say "finito!"

Winding down the play session.

Removing the conditioning collar.

Interactive play guide | 153

TEACHING AND TIMING

How does teaching and timing relate to interactive play? Through my work, helping so many different dogs and their handlers, I would say: it is not the amount of time that you spend teaching that counts, it is the quality and timing of the teaching that makes the difference. When an interactive play experience fails to reach its full potential, it a misunderstanding of this concept that is often to blame.

LEARNING TO PLAY

The common presumption is that all dogs want to play, so if a dog sees a toy he will instinctively know what to do. Because of this misconception, if a dog fails to show interest in a toy or playing, the handler will assume that the dog doesn't like to play and probably never will. The handler, therefore, gives up on creating an interactive play experience. But if we fall back on the assumption that no teaching is required, the interactive play experience will grind to a halt before it has even started.

THE VALUE OF TEACHING: A LESSON LEARNT

When I was a child I was a little overweight, and I get embarrassed if a photo taken around that time ever appears. Luckily, there was not the current obsession for documenting everything, and the photos are few and far between. At that time in my life, I was keen on food that wasn't good for me, and I was definitely not a fan of taking exercise – which was

As a handler you need to fine-tune the play experience so it has maximum benefit for your dog.

Interactive play guide | 155

not a great combination. When I went to high school, one of my P.E teachers was a mountain of a man, well over 6 ft tall with muscles on muscles. I remember having to tilt my head back and look way up when I was talking to him. He was naturally tall, but the muscles were the result of being a fitness fanatic and a former international discus thrower. One day during an athletics class, he suggested that I try throwing the discus. He probably chose me because of my bulky build, but the reason matters not. This simple request became a huge turning point in my life and I have much to thank him for. It just so happened I was OK at throwing the discus; the teacher took me under his wing and recruited me for the athletics team.

He taught me that there was more to throwing the discus than just putting my weight behind it; I needed to be fit. Initially, I was not so keen, but he introduced me to circuit workout sessions which were fun to do and left me with an amazing sense of achievement. This could not have been more different to my previous experience of exercise where I struggled round a running circuit, for what seemed like hours, feeling bored and exhausted. Little by little, he showed me how to enjoy and benefit from the exercise experience, something that, without his teaching, I would never have attempted or grown to love. My life changed for the better; I realised that I loved exercise, the weight fell off and I started to live a healthier life. To this day I still love exercise and the healthy lifestyle; I work out every day and consider my love for the exercise experience only second to my love for dogs, all because a teacher took the time to teach me.

THINK LIKE A TEACHER

Because of the common misconception that playing is something a dog will do, or should do, naturally, any type of teaching during play is often overlooked.

Compare this to my exercise experience story. When I was younger I naturally had all of the tools to exercise, but because I was never taught to adjust and adapt to an exercise routine that suited me and was enjoyable, I never tried.

But when I was taught that exercise could be an enjoyable, beneficial experience, and it could be tailor-made to suit me, I never looked back. If you and your dog don't already share an amazing interactive play experience, you have to teach him how amazing the experience can be. Interactive play is a unique experience that you and your dog can share, enjoy and benefit from. But in order to get the maximum benefit, you will need to think like a teacher and adjust and adapt your teaching techniques to show your dog how much fun he can have. Remember, you are creating an awesome, unique experience. You may now be thinking: 'that sounds great. But how can I become an amazing teacher?' Well, it's not as hard as it sounds if you focus on a single straightforward concept – adjust and adapt to develop.

ADJUST AND ADAPT TO DEVELOP

It is no coincidence that these words are used so often in this book. The words are simple, but they hold the key to thinking like a teacher. Let's start with the word develop, which seems contradictory as it's the last word in the sentence, but if you read on, it will make sense...

ALWAYS THINK TO DEVELOP

When you first start your interactive play journey, you will naturally be thinking about developing your interactive play experience, and I have no doubt that you will work on it so that it is perfect for you and your dog. However, once an interactive play experience is developing well, the handler can start to forget that, for the experience to thrive, it needs to develop. You need to ask yourself before during and after every interactive play session, how can I make this better for me and my dog? If you ask this question consistently, development will always be on your mind, which will lead to you thinking like an amazing teacher.

PUTTING THOUGHT INTO ACTION WITH ADJUSTMENTS AND ADAPTATIONS

To make thinking like a teacher even more beneficial, you need to put your thoughts into actions, and make adjustment and adaptations that will positively develop your interactive play experience. Throughout this book, I have stressed the importance of crafting your unique interactive play experience to suit you and your dog. The question you may be asking right now is: how can I adjust and adapt to suit my dog?

In fact, you hold the trump card because you know your dog better than anyone else. Why is this such an advantage? It is because you already have a great well of knowledge of the things that your dog does and doesn't like; you live with your dog and every day he will, unknowingly, give you clues about what adjustments and adaptations can be used to benefit your interactive play sessions. For example, if you have had the same toy for your dog for some time and he has shown little interest in it, there is a good chance that he is telling you that this toy doesn't suit him. The same dog may be a tea towel thief, and as amusing or annoying as this can be, this is your dog's way of telling you this toy suits him better. Our dogs will often offer us the answers on how to adjust and adapt to suit them. Adjusting and adapting your technique will play a big part in the development of your interactive play experience. It is the key to success, and often proves to be the turning point when a handler has almost given up. By remembering to adjust and adapt to develop your interactive play experience, you will not only begin think like an amazing teacher – you will become one, which will help your interactive play experience to thrive. Play seems like the most natural experience in the world but, like most things, it has to be taught first. Adopting the teacher mindset will make all the difference.

TIME AND HOW WE USE IT

More often than not, the more time that we spend doing something the better we become at it. This is also true of your interactive play experience, but there is a twist, as prolonging a play session can hinder your development. It is your dog's energy that is the deciding factor as to how much time you should spend on your interactive play sessions (see Chapter Four: Energy's Effects). You therefore need to use time to you and your dog's mutual advantage during the interactive play process. There are three factors to consider:

HOW LONG SHOULD MY INTERACTIVE PLAY SESSIONS BE?

Try to think about the quality of the experience rather than the length of time that you spend interacting. I would like you to maintain a quality over quantity mindset, and if you couple this with the conversations we had regarding energy, you will be able to judge just the right amount of time for each interactive play session.

It could be two minutes or ten minutes – the length of time makes no difference. You need to focus on the quality of the experience. You want your dog to be fully engaged in the interactive play experience, at every session, right up until the last second. For this time, nothing else matters to him except the experience that he is sharing with you. You may well find that because your interactive play experience is so mentally and physically stimulating, your dog will be just as tired after a short session as would be the case after a much longer period of conventional exercise.

HOW OFTEN SHOULD WE PLAY?

I am a big fan of little and often when it comes to interactive play, and training in general. A few short successful sessions in a day will benefit you and your dog far more than attempting one long session. Repeating play in short bursts regularly has proven itself, over and over again, to produce the best results when it comes to developing the interactive play experience.

Remember, practice makes perfect. How often you should repeat your interactive play sessions will depend on your dog's individual energy levels. Bear in mind, if your dog is tired your interactive play session will not be as good as it can be – and we are always aiming for the best quality experience. So your aim is to leave enough time between interactive play sessions so that the next session is always as energy filled and enthusiastic as the last. When should we play? The answer is related to your dog's energy levels, as you want him to have maximum energy so that you can share the best possible experience. Your superior knowledge regarding your own dog will come in handy here. For example, if you know that your dog begins to tire on a walk after 30 minutes, it would make sense to time your play session within the first ten minutes when he will be firing on all cylinders. Because you spend so much time with your dog, you will know the signs, and the times when he is bursting with energy and when he is a little jaded. So try your best to plan interactive play sessions when your dog has the most energy, and if he appears lacklustre, give it a miss. Popular times for interactive play are in the morning as part of your normal exercise routine, or after your dog has had a good period of rest. Times to avoid interactive play are at least an hour before and after meals, at the end of long walks, and at the end of a busy day. This is not to say that a dog will not play when he is tired as the desire for the experience will often override his lack of energy, but there is no doubt that the quality will suffer. By timing your play sessions when your dog has optimum energy you are setting yourself up for success.

A DIFFERENT TAKE ON TIME

As you can tell by the answers to the above questions, you need to re-evaluate your concept of time in relation to interactive play. Instead of focusing on time in the conventional sense, for example planning a five-minute interactive play session at 3 pm, you need to focus on the quality of the experience created in that time. When it comes to the timing of interactive play sessions, nothing is set in stone.

To use time most effectively, you need to become a keen observer of your dog's energy levels and focus on creating the best possible experience. If you concentrate on these two points, the duration of your sessions will grow.

TEACHING AND TIMING WRAP UP

We have now discovered how thinking like a teacher and having a slightly different perspective on time can help you to create, develop and maintain your amazing interactive play experience. I want to finish this chapter with the opening statement, as keeping this in mind will always serve you well. It is not the amount of time that you spend teaching that counts; it is the quality and timing of the teaching that makes the difference.

INCREMENTAL STEPS TO INTERACTIVITY

There is nothing wrong with thinking big, and I am a great believer in setting ambitious goals to achieve with my dogs, and in life in general.

However, there are times when we become so focused on the big goal, we overlook the process of getting there and become daunted by the task. But I have found that when you plan and love the process, the big goal always comes sooner than expected – and you will love every step of the journey.

When a skilled mason builds a brick wall, he makes a clear plan and then lays some strong foundations.

Once this is done he can focus on laying each brick, as perfectly as possible, one at a time. Before long the masterpiece is complete and will stand the test of time.

If you focus on creating the whole interactive play experience in one go, you are likely to become overwhelmed. It is so much better to have a clear vision of a perfect interactive play experience, and then make a plan of how to create it.

Then you can work towards creating your masterpiece, a brick at a time.

Picture your end goal, but build your interactive play experience brick by brick.

interactive play guide | 163

THE BRICK BY BRICK BENEFITS FOR YOU AND YOUR DOG

To achieve your perfect interactive play experience, both you and your dog will need to develop, albeit in different ways. Starting with the dog: it will probably be his desire and drive for the new experience that needs to develop.

By reducing these drives and desires into specific bricks, and working on them one at a time, you will produce the best lasting results. This brick by brick approach will not only benefit the dog, but also the handler.

To develop the specific drives and desires of his dog, the handler will need to work on his own interactive play skills, as well as his understanding of his dog, to create the interactive play experience. By working on these areas, one brick at a time, the handler will be honing one skill at a time.

Steady progress means that a skill will become second nature before the handler moves on to the next brick in the wall. It is then far easier to tackle the next skill rather than trying to work on the entire skill set at one go. So let's work out a brick by brick plan to create your amazing interactive play experience.

PICTURE YOUR END GOAL

How are you going to use your interactive play experience to benefit you and your dog's life? Is it to be practised regularly to build the relationship that you share with your dog, maybe as part of your exercise routine?

Or do you have a specialist requirement for your interactive play experience; for example, you want to use it as a reward during training for your chosen discipline. Or maybe it's both.

Your preference will be personal – it's all about what you want from your dog – but it is important to make up your mind so you can form a vision of your interactive play end goal.

If your play is to build your relationship with your dog, using it as part of your existing exercise programme, your end goal may be to use the interactive play collar so you can enjoy the experience at your leisure and as you please. Alternatively, perhaps your end goal is to use your interactive play experience in short bursts for numerous rewards while training your dog, which may be preferable to giving food.

These are just examples of what you can do; your end goal will be specific to you and your dog. But once you have a clear idea of what you want to achieve, you can make a step-by-step plan of how to get there.

WHERE ARE YOU NOW?

The first step is to work out where you are now in comparison to your end goal. Perhaps you had never heard of interactive play before reading this book and your end goal is to create an interactive play experience that you and your dog can enjoy on a regular basis.

If this is the case, you are beginning a brand new journey and you can use the information we have discussed to start the process.

Alternatively, you may be training your dog for a specific activity and rewarding with a toy, but you are experiencing problems with toy possession. If this is the case, you will be aiming to establish interactive play where the dog is focusing on you rather than running off with his toy to entertain himself.

By thinking about where you are in comparison to your end

goal, you will be able to decide how you are going to use this information and your new interactive play skills to get to get where you want to be. You are going to think like a teacher and decide what you have got to do to reach your goal.

BUILDING BRICK BY BRICK

Once you know what you want to achieve, you need break down the process and then start building brick by brick. Planning incrementally, in this way, will give you a structured route to help you reach your goal. Let's imagine you want to use interactive play to enhance your relationship with your dog, but your dog shows little interest in the toys you offer.

To achieve your end goal, your first step – or your first brick in the wall – is to get your dog interested and engaged with an interactive play toy. How can you achieve this? At this stage, your end goal may seem very distant, but if you break down the process, it is not so daunting.

The planned steps could be:

1. Check out Chapter Three (Toy Selection) to consider whether you have chosen toys that are suitable for your dog, and make adjustments accordingly.

2. Use the information in Chapter Six (Activating The Toy) to create or refine your activation process so that it suits your dog and he is ready engage the toy.

3. Consider the information in Chapter Four (Energy's Effects) to make sure you are using your energy and your dog's energy in the best way so that it benefits your activation process.

4. Work out how took to develop your dog's toy activation response (TAR), by looking at all the information provided in the book, and then adjusting and adapting it to suit your dog.

5. Stack all the odds in your favour by focusing on short successful sessions, making sure you always finish on a win.

6. Develop your dog's toy activation response (TAR) until he consistently and enthusiastically engages the toy at every session. If you follow this plan, you now have a dog that is ready to play with a toy, and you can move on to the next stage – or the next brick in the wall – on the journey to achieving your end goal.

GO FOR A LITTLE WIN AT EVERY SESSION

Focusing on achieving a little win at every session has proved, time and again, to be beneficial for interactive play development. What do I mean by a little win?

Let's look at the example above where the dog has little or no interest in the toy. If, by the end of the first session, the dog shows enough interest to engage the toy that you have chosen during the activation process, you have achieved your little win.

This may seem like a small step – and it is – but it is a successful winning step that has positively developed your interactive play experience. By focusing on achieving little wins at every session, your interactive play experience will develop, moving in the right direction so you will reach your end goal far quicker than if you tried to get to the end goal in one go.

These little wins work in two ways: the dog feels he has had a positive experience – and so does the handler. In terms of building confidence, this is of equal importance to both dog and handler.

As the dog's desires and drives develop he, increasingly, wants to play, and the handler, buoyed up by the dog's response, hones the skills needed for interactive play. Remember, interactive play is a shared experience so both handler and dog

This Labrador has no natural enthusiasm for a game.

Working at a distance, an activation extension incites some interest.

168 | Interactive play guide

The Labrador is more committed and is ready to interact close at hand.

Now he truly wants to play.

Interactive play guide | 169

Time to work without the help of the activation extension.

When the toy is activated, the Labrador is keen to engage.

Interactive play has now become highly desirable.

End of the session and time for a fair trade swap.

Interactive play guide | 171

need to develop to create the best possible experience.

The results for both dog and handler are easy to see as the commitment to engage and the quality of play improves. In addition, the relationship between dog and handler is strengthening with every session. It's a win win situation – and lots of little winning sessions like this will help you to achieve lasting results.

USE CONSISTENCY FOR CEMENT

If you think of each step to creating your interactive play experience as bricks in a wall, you will need cement to secure the bricks – and this means applying consistency. Let me explain.

Once you have broken your end vision down into as many bricks as possible, you need to focus on achieving consistency on the first brick before moving on to the next.

So looking at the dog who is ready to play and engage the toy, you now need to keep working until he is actively interested in the toy every time it is activated and consistently engages with it.

It is tempting to move on to the next brick with the first sign of success, but it is far more beneficial to focus on achieving the result consistently before moving on. Inevitably, results will be sporadic as you both develop and adjust to the new experience.

For example, there may be a session when your dog is super interested and engages the toy the second it is activated with boundless enthusiasm, and then you may have another session when he does not seem so keen.

You need focus on a consistent response from your dog before moving on, as his inconsistent response is telling you that his desires and drives have not developed sufficiently to move on to the next brick.

The only way to get this response consistently is through adjusting and adapting, and with regular practice. Once you have a consistent response you can start to work on the next brick, again using consistency as cement.

WHEN YOUR SESSION DOESN'T GO TO PLAN

What happens when a session fails to go according to plan? This is something that happens to all teachers, and is even more relevant when you are working with an animal.

However, there is no need to despair as the incremental approach can be a real help in this situation. I have divided my strategy into three basic steps:

1. Make sure that the session finishes on a little win of some sort; it doesn't matter how small it is, just make sure the session finishes on a positive experience for you and your dog.

2. Once the session is over, try to work out why the session didn't go to plan. For example, was it a problem with energy levels, with a new environment, or with the task you were asking for? If you give it some thought, you will generally find there is a reason for your dog's response.

3. Work out how to adjust and adapt your methodology so you can eradicate the cause and overcome the issue at your next session.

Another benefit of adopting this incremental approach when a session does not go well is that it will make pinpointing the cause much easier. Why is that?

If you are focusing on one brick at a time rather than attempting

You and your dog are learning all the time...

to achieve the end goal at one go, you will become very familiar with your dog's behaviour. As you develop and create the play process, you will find out what works for him and what doesn't, what he likes and what he doesn't like.

Through your shared experience, you will acquire a unique understanding of your dog which will make it so much easier to pinpoint the reason for setbacks that may occur.

With this knowledge, you will then be able to adjust and adapt what you are doing to overcome the problem and create the best possible experience.

THE BRICKS ARE ALL IN PLACE

We have talked through all the benefits, for both you and your dog, of adopting the incremental approach to creating your interactive play experience.

But what I have not mentioned is how quickly this allows you to reach your end goal. If you focus on every brick, and position each brick with total consistency, you will not only achieve the goal you want in record time – you will also love the process.

VOCALISATION CONSIDERATIONS

What do I mean by vocalisation considerations and how do they relate to your interactive play experience?

When I am teaching, I am regularly reminded of the fact that, as humans, dog lovers, and trainers, we rely on our voices or vocalisation to stimulate our dogs in a variety of circumstances.

There is no doubt that vocalisation is a valuable tool when training dogs, but as with every other tool, we need to learn how to use it to best advantage.

I have seen verbal communication achieve some great results but, equally, I have seen how excessive vocalisation can work against developing drives and desires in many dogs, and can ultimately hinder creating an amazing interactive play experience.

Why is that? Generally, it is because verbal communication has moved from being a highly useful tool to becoming a crutch that is overused, often at times when it is not even needed. In this chapter we will talk through simple steps which will show you how to get the best from talking to your dog.

HOW A CRUTCH CAN BECOME A COMPLICATION?

I am often called on to help dog trainers who take part in competitive dog sports ranging from heelwork to music to

We love to talk – but too much vocalisation can be a hindrance when you are communicating with your dog.

Interactive play guide | 177

working sports. I begin every consultation asking: how can I help?

A common response is that the dog's drive and focus is fantastic in training, but it fades during competition. Many of my clients use interactive play as a reward during their training, so the first thing I do is watch how they play with their dog. One factor often becomes apparent; the amount of vocalisation that is used by the handler to initiate and partake in the play experience is overwhelming.

Vocalisation has become a crutch and, in many cases, the dog has been conditioned to need this high degree of vocalisation in order to maintain focus.

This rapidly becomes a problem when competing, as minimal vocalisation is either mandatory or preferred in many dog sports. It is therefore obvious why a dog performs like a rock star in training but struggles during competition.

If you have been using your voice as a crutch during your interactive play experience, don't panic. You can incrementally reduce the amount of vocalisation, and only use your voice when it is beneficial or necessary.

In this book we have talked through the interactive play skills you need, and as your play experience develops, so will the application of these skills. In time you will find that there is less and less need to use your voice as you have the skills to cope without it.

TO SPEAK OR NOT TO SPEAK?

It is far better to use your voice only when it is necessary and beneficial to the development of your dog and your interactive play experience. In this way your voice is an asset rather than turning into a version of white noise.

Instead of relying on a constant stream of vocalisation, use your voice to pinpoint words for positive reinforcement, to praise your dog, and for selective encouragement or conditioned cue words. In this way, you are using vocalisation as a positive means of developing your interactive play experience.

A FORM OF WHITE NOISE

When I hear a song that I really like, I am guilty of playing it over and over again. It gets to the point when I know all the words and I am so familiar with it that I almost stop listening: the words have lost their effect.

Excessive vocalisation during interactive play produces similar results in our dogs. In some cases it may become a crutch, but it is equally likely to become a form of white noise.

What do I mean by white noise? This is when vocalisation is used so much that the dog hears the noise on one frequency and the words are meaningless.

He cannot distinguish between important verbal communication, such as praise or a cue word, and the never-ending flow of vocalisation, which often becomes louder and louder as play progresses. The typical scenario is that the dog switches off and the handler finishes the session with a sore throat!

VOCALISATION ASSOCIATIONS

The associations that your dog has with your voice can prove to be a hugely beneficial part of your interactive play experience. For example, if you have taught your dog to love to let go, your cue and pinpoint words are massively beneficial as part of your interactive play experience.

However, there are also times when the associations that your dog has with your voice can work against you. Let me explain.

We have just talked about how over-using vocalisation can become another form of white noise to your dog during the interactive play experience.

But there is the opposite end of the scale; this is when a dog is super-responsive to his handler's voice, which can often be the case with dogs that take part in a lot of training. It presents as an issue if the handler vocalises at the wrong time.

This is most likely to occur when you are developing the play experience; everything is brand new to your dog and his desire for the activity has yet to be established. In this situation, the handler vocalises and the dog releases the toy presenting a pre-conditioned behaviour or seeking a reward.

This makes developing the dog's desires, and the overall interactive play experience, challenging because he is learning to love to let go at the wrong time.

For the many dogs that are highly food driven, or have done lots of food-based training, the association of the handler's voice with food rewards produces further problems.

When the handler speaks the dog loses interest in the interactive play process and goes through all manner of pre-learnt tricks and behaviours to get a food reward. At this stage, the dog is new to the play experience and does not realise how rewarding it can be.

Understandably, the handler assumes his dog is not interested in interactive play, and gives up. However, if the handler reduced the amount of vocalisation, the issue would not arise, which would allow them to create their own unique experience.

FUZZY THINKING

Excessive vocalisation on the part of the handler can also drive a dog to be so stimulated that he falls prey to fuzzy thinking. I use this term because the dog becomes so excited, and overly stimulated, that he is unable to focus on any task, including play. Fuzzy thinking behaviour will take the form of excessive barking, spinning in circles and jumping up; the dog does not know what to do or how to channel his energy.

I see this as a waste of energy; a failure on the part of us handlers to capitalise on the dog's enthusiasm, which should be used to benefit the interactive play experience.

The dog responds to the level of vocalisation and goes into fuzzy thinking mode; an association is formed and fuzzy thinking behaviour is the result. But if the handler reduces the vocalisation, the dog will come out of the fuzzy thinking mind state with a clearer head and will be able to fully enjoy the interactive play experience.

VOCALISATION EVALUATION

Vocalisation is a blessing and curse: it can be the making of your interactive play experience or it can damage it to the point when the experience founders and fails to develop. The golden rule is to only use your voice when it is necessary and when it will benefit your dog and your interactive play process. Let your interactive play skills do the rest.

182 | Interactive play guide

If you avoid fuzzy thinking, your dog has a clear picture of what you want from him.

interactive play guide | 183

EVERY DOG IS UNIQUE

Every dog has his own unique DNA, which plays a big role in moulding the temperament and characteristics that we come to love. Your dog's unique character will play a big part in creating your interactive play experience and is something I really want you to embrace.

LOOKS RARELY PAINT THE WHOLE PICTURE

On occasion, I have had two puppies from the same litter at one of my interactive play workshops. They are often very similar in looks, and both are equally gorgeous, but it serves as an important reminder that every dog is unique.

Before we begin a workshop, I make a point of talking to the students so I can find out a bit about their dogs.

On this particular occasion, the owner of one of the littermates said that their puppy was not as interested in play as his sibling. Both owners were introducing play in exactly the same way, which was working really well for one pup but not so well for the other. When I started working with each of the puppies, one to one, it became clear that their similarity in looks was not painting the whole picture.

The first of the puppies I worked with had a naturally high

You need to look beyond stereotypes of breed type and tune into your dog's unique personality.

Interactive play guide | 185

toy activation response level, and had taken really well to his owner's arm's length toy activation technique.

The second puppy's natural toy activation response level was not as high as her sibling's and she was also a big fan of affection and cuddles in particular.

When her owner attempted the same arm's length activation process, the toy failed to attract her interest. After a couple of attempts at mouthing the toy, she opted for a cuddle from her owner – to the mutual delight of both puppy and owner.

This had become a habit and the puppy had started to associate the toy being produced with a cuddle, which was slowing the creation of their interactive play experience. We adjusted and adapted the activation process with the use of an activation extension and a different toy.

The owner was astonished by the difference in the puppy, who changed from showing little interest in the toy, or in interactive play, to displaying the same focus and intensity for her new toy as her sibling – all in a very short period of time.

By adjusting and adapting the play process to suit the individual, the interactive play experience could now develop and thrive.

So, no matter how similar two dogs may seem, every dog is unique. As a handler you need to think on your feet: what works for one dog may not work for another, and you may be one minor adjustment away from creating your amazing unique interactive play experience.

Try to keep this in mind when you are interacting with your dog – and bear in mind what could have happened if both puppy owners had continued to use the same techniques.

THINK OUTSIDE OF THE BOX AND EMBRACE UNIQUE

During the course of this book we have talked about the fundamentals of creating an amazing and unique interactive play experience; we have also discussed the importance of adjusting and adapting your techniques to suit you and your dog.

You need to employ the fundamentals when creating your experience but when you are adjusting and adapting, you need to be versatile, creative, and willing to think outside the box.

Focus on what will work best for you and your dog as this is the essence of creating and sharing a unique interactive play experience. We have talked through lots of examples of how I have helped owners to embrace their dog's unique traits and adjust and adapt to create their interactive play experience – now it is up to you. You have the knowledge, the skills and the love for dogs to put it all into action.

Just as you love our dog's own unique character, you will love your own amazing unique interactive play experience. Remember what works for you and your dog is always the right answer.

LOVE THE JOURNEY

I wrote this book because I want to share this unique and amazing interactive play experience, and all its benefits, with as many dog lovers and their dogs as possible. I hope that you embark on an interactive mission and love the journey that it takes you on.

The reason I feel so passionately about spreading the word is because I have seen first hand, on many occasions, how this unique type of interactive play has helped so many dog lovers and their dogs, with a wide variety of needs.

Interactive play helps owners and their dogs overcome behavioural problems, it enhances dog/owner relationships, it is a vital tool in training, and it is a brilliant way to have fun with your dog. I receive lots of emails and messages from people who ask for advice on how to turn their existing play into an amazing interactive play experience.

I hope this book provides all the information you need, and serves as an easy-to-access reference that you can use while creating your own unique interactive play experience.

Interactive, in this instance, means you and your dog influencing or having an effect on each other. All too often you hear of a dog that has dozens of toys gathering dust in a corner; he has little interest in his toys, and no interest in playing with his owner.

But if you find one toy that suits your dog, and develop the skills outlined in this book, you will create an amazing interactive play experience. Remember, with a little interactive input, you can turn rags to riches.

Never under-estimate the power of interactive play.

Interactive play guide | 189

THE NEXT STEP

As you embark on the exciting journey of creating an interactive play experience, you will not only have lots of fun, you will also develop a better understanding of your dog and enhance the relationship you share with him. But this is not where the benefits of interactive play stop. Let me explain:

I am lucky enough to work with hundreds of dogs and their owners every year. Whether I am working with a pet Yorkshire Terrier that enjoys quiet nights in front of the fire, a Border Collie that adores agility training or a Malinois that likes to fight crime, there is a common thread that can present a challenge.

This may take different forms, but it always relates to the owner struggling to communicate with their dog when he is stimulated or excited.

Through no fault of his own, a dog that is over-aroused starts to display undesirable behaviour. For example, the agility mad Border Collie decides to chase the dog in the neighbouring ring, apparently forgetting all of the hours that you have spent training his recall. Why is that?

Very often, the reason is that most owners have little practice when it comes to interacting or communicating with their dogs when they are stimulated or excited, and therefore find themselves at a loss. This is where the interactive play experience comes in.

During your interactive play sessions, you are not only creating your dog's favourite experience, you are stimulating him. This provides the ideal opportunity to practise communicating with your dog when he in a heightened emotional state. In addition, it teaches him to focus on you – even when he is highly excited – because you are the creator of the most amazing experience.

Interactive play helps to position you at the centre of your dog's world, and it also gives you the huge of advantage of practising your communication skills when your dog is aroused.

This will be of great benefit in many ways, but most particularly with regard to your dog's responsiveness and his ability to focus in stimulating situations – and the best part is that you and your dog will be have lots of fun the whole time.

I will be expanding on this in my next book, giving you advice and information so you can use interactive play to communicate clearly with your dog when he is super excited.

In the meantime, I hope you will use all of the information in this book to build and develop your own play experience. More importantly, I want you to love the journey because, believe me, it will be just as much fun as the destination.

For the widest selection of toys and training aids at the most competitive prices, check out the following websites.

UK & EUROPE

www.performancedog.co.uk

www.positiveanimalsolutions.com

UNITED STATES

www.dogwise.com

www.cleanrun.com